EATING CLEAN

DELICIOUS WHOLE FOOD RECIPES

Publications International, Ltd.

CONTENTS

INTRODUCTION 4

SLOW COOKING TIPS 6

BREAKFAST 10

SOUPS AND CHILIES 42

VEGETARIAN 80

MAIN DISHES 118

SIDES 156

INDEX 188

METRIC CONVERSION CHART 192

INTRODUCTION

EATING CLEAN

Eating clean is not a "diet" in the typical sense; that is, it's not a crash diet. You don't have to eliminate a food group, count calories, eat like a caveman or avoid fat. The principles of clean eating are quite simple—eat foods in their natural state (or as close as possible) and avoid processed foods, refined sugars (white sugar), refined grains (white flour) and high-sodium foods—but it does take planning and commitment to implement them into your life.

Start by going through your pantry and getting rid of anything that's old or processed: half boxes of stale cereal, high-sodium soups, packaged cookies, and that one sleeve of crackers left over from your holiday party.

Plan your meals, make a list and then go grocery shopping with fresh eyes and plenty of time to read labels and explore. Pay particular attention to the produce section of your grocery store; you may be surprised to find things you've never seen before.

Keep in mind that not everything from a jar or can is bad. Look at the ingredients for many jarred salsas and you'll find that they're simply tomatoes, vegetables and seasonings. Jarred fruit packed in water, like peach slices, pineapple chunks and grapefruit sections, make it easy to snack on fruit when fresh versions are not available or you don't have time to prepare it. Organic canned beans, tomatoes and vegetables are readily available and make meal preparations much easier.

TIPS AND SUGGESTIONS

- Eat small meals throughout the day to keep your blood sugar and energy levels steady. If you're not going to be at home or work, pack a cooler bag with a snack. Smoothies and juices make great pick-me-ups on the run; make them in the morning and transport them in a jar or travel mug.

- Use clean eating as an opportunity to make other positive lifestyle changes: start (or continue) exercising, drink lots of water and get plenty of sleep.

- Be realistic. It's easy to be overwhelmed by too many rules and criteria when beginning a new eating plan, so start small and make gradual changes. When you run out of regular pasta and white rice, buy whole wheat pasta and brown rice next time. Choose oats, granola and dried fruit instead of breakfast cereal. If you take sugar in your coffee or tea, gradually reduce the amount you use until you don't need it anymore.

- Use common sense when shopping. If a product has a lot of ingredients, any of them sugar and most of them unpronounceable, skip it.

- When shopping for fruits, vegetables, meats and dairy, choose organic or the best quality that you can afford. Try farmers' markets for eggs and cheese, and look for produce marked "local" at the grocery store for just-picked freshness.

QUICK REFERENCE GUIDE TO GROCERY SHOPPING

STOCK UP

VEGETABLES, ALL KINDS
fresh
frozen
canned

FRUIT, ALL KINDS
fresh
frozen
canned or jarred
dried

WHOLE GRAINS
barley
oats
quinoa
rice (brown)
whole grain pasta

PROTEIN
beans
beef
chicken
eggs
fish and shellfish
lamb
pork
tofu
turkey

DAIRY
butter
dairy-free milk
  alternatives (soymilk,
  coconut milk, almond
  milk, rice milk)
milk
yogurt (plain)

NUTS AND OILS
avocado oil
coconut oil
nuts (all kinds)
nut butters
olive oil
seeds (chia, flax,
  pumpkin, sesame,
  sunflower)

SEASONINGS AND SAUCES
herbs (fresh and dried)
hot sauce
mustard
sea salt and black
  pepper
spices
vinegar

SWEETENERS
agave nectar
honey
maple syrup

PANTRY STAPLES
broth
canned beans
canned tomatoes and
  tomato sauce
coconut milk
salsa

AVOID

PROCESSED FOODS
canned soups
chips and pretzels
fat-free dairy products
frozen pizza and meals
hot dogs
margarine
packaged shredded
  cheese
salad dressings

REFINED GRAINS
crackers
packaged breads
regular pasta
white rice

SUGAR
artificial sugar substitute
candy
cookies
ice cream
jams and jellies
sweetened peanut
  butter
soda, energy drinks and
  other sugary beverages
sugary cereals
yogurt with added sugar

BRAISED CHIPOTLE BEEF
P. 138

SIZES OF CROCK-POT® SLOW COOKERS

Smaller **CROCK-POT®** slow cookers—such as 1- to 3½-quart models—are the perfect size for cooking for singles, a couple or empty nesters (and also for serving dips).

While medium-size **CROCK-POT®** slow cookers (those holding somewhere between 3 quarts and 5 quarts) will easily cook enough food at one time to feed a small family, they are also convenient for holiday side dishes or appetizers.

Large **CROCK-POT®** slow cookers are great for large family dinners, holiday entertaining and potluck suppers. A 6- to 7-quart model is ideal if you like to make meals in advance. Or, have dinner tonight and store leftovers for later.

TYPES OF CROCK-POT® SLOW COOKERS

Current **CROCK-POT®** slow cookers come equipped with many different features and benefits, from auto cook programs to oven-safe stoneware to timed programming. Please visit **WWW.CROCK-POT.COM** to find the **CROCK-POT®** slow cooker that best suits your needs.

How you plan to use a **CROCK-POT®** slow cooker may affect the model you choose to purchase. For everyday cooking, choose a size large enough to serve your family. If you plan to use the **CROCK-POT®** slow cooker primarily for entertaining, choose one of the larger sizes. Basic **CROCK-POT®** slow cookers can hold as little as 16 ounces or as much as 7 quarts. The smallest sizes are great for keeping dips warm on a buffet, while the larger sizes can more readily fit large quantities of food and larger roasts.

COOKING, STIRRING AND FOOD SAFETY

CROCK-POT® slow cookers are safe to leave unattended. The outer heating base may get hot as it cooks, but it should not pose a fire hazard. The heating element in the heating base functions at a low wattage and is safe for your countertops.

Your **CROCK-POT®** slow cooker should be filled about one-half to three-fourths full for most recipes unless otherwise instructed. Lean meats such as chicken or pork tenderloin will cook faster than meats with more connective tissue and fat such as beef chuck or pork shoulder. Bone-in meats will take longer than boneless cuts. Typical **CROCK-POT®** slow cooker dishes take approximately 7 to 8 hours to reach the simmer point on LOW and about 3 to 4 hours on HIGH. Once the vegetables and meat start to simmer and braise, their flavors will fully blend and meat will become fall-off-the-bone tender.

According to the U.S. Department of Agriculture, all bacteria are killed at a temperature of 165°F. It's important to follow the recommended cooking times and not to open the lid often, especially early in the cooking process when heat is building up inside the unit. If you need to open the lid to check on your food or are adding additional ingredients, remember to allow additional cooking time if necessary to ensure food is cooked through and tender.

Large **CROCK-POT**® slow cookers, the 6- to 7-quart sizes, may benefit from a quick stir halfway through cook time to help distribute heat and promote even cooking. It's usually unnecessary to stir at all, as even ½ cup liquid will help to distribute heat, and the stoneware is the perfect medium for holding food at an even temperature throughout the cooking process.

OVEN-SAFE STONEWARE

All **CROCK-POT**® slow cooker removable stoneware inserts may (without their lids) be used safely in ovens at up to 400°F. In addition, all **CROCK-POT**® slow cookers are microwavable without their lids. If you own another slow cooker brand, please refer to your owner's manual for specific stoneware cooking medium tolerances.

FROZEN FOOD

Frozen food can be successfully cooked in a **CROCK-POT**® slow cooker. However, it will require a longer cooking time than the same recipe made with fresh food. Using an instant-read thermometer is recommended to ensure meat is fully cooked.

PASTA AND RICE

If you are converting a recipe for your **CROCK-POT**® slow cooker that calls for uncooked pasta, first cook the pasta on the stovetop just until slightly tender. Then add the pasta to the **CROCK-POT**® slow cooker.

If you are converting a recipe for the **CROCK-POT**® slow cooker that calls for cooked rice, stir in raw rice with the other recipe ingredients plus ¼ cup extra liquid per ¼ cup of raw rice.

BEANS

Beans must be softened completely before combining with sugar and/or acidic foods in the **CROCK-POT**® slow cooker. Sugar and acid have a hardening effect on beans and will prevent softening. Fully cooked canned beans may be used as a substitute for dried beans.

VEGETABLES

Root vegetables often cook more slowly than meat. Cut vegetables accordingly to cook at the same rate as meat—large versus small or lean versus marbled— and place near the sides or bottom of the stoneware to facilitate cooking.

HERBS

Fresh herbs add flavor and color when added at the end of the cooking cycle; if added at the beginning, many fresh herbs' flavor will dissipate over long cook times. Ground and/or dried herbs and spices work well in slow cooking and may be added at the beginning of cook time. For dishes with shorter cook times, hearty fresh herbs such as rosemary and thyme hold up well. The flavor power of all herbs and spices can vary greatly depending on their particular strength and shelf life. Use chili powders and garlic powder sparingly, as these can sometimes intensify over the long cook times. Always taste the finished dish and correct seasonings including salt and pepper.

LIQUIDS

It is not necessary to use more than ½ to 1 cup liquid in most instances. Most juices in meats and vegetables are retained more in slow cooking than in conventional cooking. Excess liquid can be cooked down and concentrated after slow cooking, either on the stovetop or by removing the meat and vegetables from the stoneware. Then stirring in one of the following thickeners and setting the **CROCK-POT**® slow cooker to HIGH. Cover and cook the liquid on HIGH for approximately 15 minutes or until thickened.

FLOUR: All-purpose flour is often used to thicken soups or stews. Stir water into the flour in a small bowl until smooth. With the **CROCK-POT**® slow cooker on HIGH, whisk flour mixture into the liquid in the **CROCK-POT**® slow cooker. Cover; cook on HIGH 15 minutes or until the mixture is thickened.

CORNSTARCH: Cornstarch gives sauces a clear, shiny appearance; it's used most often for sweet dessert sauces and stir-fry sauces. Stir water into the

cornstarch in a small bowl until the cornstarch is dissolved. Quickly stir this mixture into the liquid in the **CROCK-POT**® slow cooker; the sauce will thicken as soon as the liquid simmers. Cornstarch breaks down with too much heat, so never add it at the beginning of the slow cooking process and turn off the heat as soon as the sauce thickens.

MILK

Milk, cream and sour cream break down during extended cooking. When possible, add them during the last 15 to 30 minutes of slow cooking, until just heated through. Condensed soups may be substituted for milk and may cook for extended times.

FISH

Fish is delicate and should be stirred into the **CROCK-POT**® slow cooker gently during the last 15 to 30 minutes of cooking. Cover; cook just until cooked through and serve immediately.

SIMPLE SALMON WITH FRESH SALSA
P. 142

BREAKFAST

WHOA BREAKFAST

MAKES 6 SERVINGS

3 cups water

2 cups chopped peeled apples

1½ cups steel-cut or old-fashioned oats

¼ cup sliced almonds

½ teaspoon ground cinnamon

Combine water, apples, oats, almonds and cinnamon in **CROCK-POT®** slow cooker. Cover; cook on LOW 8 hours.

GINGER PEAR CIDER

MAKES 8 TO 10 SERVINGS

8 cups unsweetened pear juice

¾ cup fresh lemon juice

¼ to ½ cup honey

10 whole cloves

2 whole cinnamon sticks, plus additional for garnish

8 slices fresh ginger

1. Combine pear juice, lemon juice, honey, cloves, 2 cinnamon sticks and ginger in 5-quart **CROCK-POT**® slow cooker.

2. Cover; cook on LOW 5 to 6 hours or on HIGH 2½ to 3 hours. Remove and discard cloves, cinnamon sticks and ginger before serving. Garnish with additional cinnamon sticks.

MEDITERRANEAN FRITTATA

MAKES 4 TO 6 SERVINGS

Butter, softened

3 tablespoons extra virgin olive oil

1 large onion, chopped

2 cups (8 ounces) sliced mushrooms

6 cloves garlic, sliced

1 teaspoon dried basil

1 medium red bell pepper, chopped

1 package (10 ounces) frozen chopped spinach, thawed and squeezed dry

¼ cup sliced kalamata olives

8 eggs, beaten

4 ounces feta cheese, crumbled

½ teaspoon salt

¼ teaspoon black pepper

1. Coat inside of 5- to 6-quart **CROCK-POT®** slow cooker with butter. Heat oil in large skillet over medium-high heat. Add onion, mushrooms, garlic and basil; cook and stir 2 to 3 minutes or until slightly softened. Add bell pepper; cook 4 to 5 minutes or until vegetables are tender. Stir in spinach; cook 2 minutes. Stir in olives. Remove onion mixture to **CROCK-POT®** slow cooker.

2. Combine eggs, cheese, salt and black pepper in large bowl. Pour over vegetables in **CROCK-POT®** slow cooker. Cover; cook on LOW 2½ to 3 hours or on HIGH 1½ to 2 hours or until eggs are set. Cut into wedges to serve.

 **BREAKFAST**

OVERNIGHT BREAKFAST PORRIDGE

MAKES 4 SERVINGS

- ¾ cup steel-cut oats
- ¼ cup uncooked quinoa, rinsed and drained
- ¼ cup dried cranberries, plus additional for serving
- ¼ cup raisins
- 3 tablespoons ground flax seeds
- 2 tablespoons chia seeds
- ¼ teaspoon ground cinnamon
- 2½ cups almond milk, plus additional for serving

  Maple syrup (optional)
- ¼ cup sliced almonds, toasted*

To toast almonds, spread in single layer in heavy skillet. Cook and stir over medium heat 1 to 2 minutes or until nuts are lightly browned.

1. Combine oats, quinoa, ¼ cup cranberries, raisins, flax seeds, chia seeds and cinnamon in heat-safe bowl that fits inside of 5- or 6-quart **CROCK-POT**® slow cooker. Stir in 2½ cups almond milk.

2. Place bowl in **CROCK-POT**® slow cooker; pour enough water to come halfway up side of bowl.

3. Cover; cook on LOW 8 hours. Carefully remove bowl from **CROCK-POT**® slow cooker. Stir in additional almond milk, if desired. Top each serving with maple syrup, almonds and additional cranberries, if desired.

MULLED CRAN-APPLE JUICE

MAKES 8 SERVINGS

- 1 orange
- 1 lemon
- 1 lime
- 15 whole black peppercorns
- 10 whole cloves
- 10 whole allspice
- 3 whole cinnamon sticks, plus additional for garnish
- 1 (5-inch) square double-thickness cheesecloth
- 6 cups unsweetened apple juice
- 3 cups unsweetened cranberry juice
- 3 tablespoons maple syrup

1. Use vegetable peeler to remove 5 to 6 (2- to 3-inch-long) sections of orange, lemon and lime peel, being careful to avoid white pith. Squeeze juice from orange, set juice aside.

2. Place peels, peppercorns, cloves, allspice and 3 cinnamon sticks in center of cheesecloth. Bring corners together; tie with cotton string or strip of additional cheesecloth.

3. Pour apple juice, cranberry juice, maple syrup and reserved orange juice into 5-quart **CROCK-POT®** slow cooker; add spice bag. Cover; cook on LOW 5 to 6 hours or on HIGH 2½ to 3 hours. Remove and discard spice bag. Serve with additional cinnamon sticks.

OATMEAL WITH MAPLE-GLAZED APPLES AND CRANBERRIES

MAKES 4 SERVINGS

- 3 **cups water**
- 2 **cups quick-cooking or old-fashioned oats**
- ¼ **teaspoon salt**
- 1 **teaspoon unsalted butter**
- 2 **medium red or Golden Delicious apples, unpeeled and cut into ½-inch pieces**
- ¼ **teaspoon ground cinnamon**
- 2 **tablespoons maple syrup**
- ¼ **cup dried cranberries**

1. Combine water, oats and salt in **CROCK-POT**® slow cooker. Cover; cook on LOW 8 hours.

2. Melt butter in large nonstick skillet over medium heat. Add apples and cinnamon; cook and stir 4 to 5 minutes or until tender. Stir in maple syrup; heat through.

3. Top each oatmeal serving evenly with apple mixture and dried cranberries.

SPICED APPLE TEA

MAKES 4 SERVINGS

3 bags cinnamon herbal tea

3 cups boiling water

2 cups unsweetened apple juice

6 whole cloves

1 whole cinnamon stick

1. Place tea bags in **CROCK-POT**® slow cooker. Pour boiling water over tea bags; cover and let steep 10 minutes. Remove and discard tea bags.

2. Add apple juice, cloves and cinnamon stick to **CROCK-POT**® slow cooker. Cover; cook on LOW 2 to 3 hours. Remove and discard cloves and cinnamon stick. Serve warm in mugs.

FOUR FRUIT OATMEAL

MAKES 4 SERVINGS

4¼ cups water

1 cup steel-cut oats

⅓ cup golden raisins

⅓ cup dried cranberries

⅓ cup dried cherries

2 tablespoons honey

1 teaspoon vanilla

¼ teaspoon salt

1 cup fresh sliced strawberries

Combine water, oats, raisins, cranberries, cherries, honey, vanilla and salt in **CROCK-POT**® slow cooker; stir to blend. Cover; cook on LOW 7 to 7½ hours. Top each serving evenly with strawberries.

BRAN MUFFIN BREAD

MAKES 1 LOAF

¼ cup (½ stick) unsalted butter, melted, plus additional for mold

2 cups whole wheat flour, plus additional for mold*

2 cups all-bran cereal

2 teaspoons baking powder

1 teaspoon baking soda

½ teaspoon salt

¼ teaspoon ground cinnamon

1 egg

1½ cups buttermilk

¼ cup molasses

1 cup chopped walnuts

½ cup raisins

Fresh fruit (optional)

Honey (optional)

For proper texture of finished bread, spoon flour into measuring cup and level off. Do not dip into bag, pack down flour or tap on counter to level when measuring.

1. Butter and flour 8-cup mold that fits inside of 6-quart **CROCK-POT®** slow cooker; set aside. Combine cereal, 2 cups flour, baking powder, baking soda, salt and cinnamon in large bowl; stir to blend.

2. Beat egg in medium bowl. Add buttermilk, molasses and ¼ cup melted butter; stir to blend. Add buttermilk mixture to flour mixture; stir just until combined. Stir in walnuts and raisins. Spoon batter into prepared mold. Cover with buttered foil, butter side down.

3. Place rack in **CROCK-POT®** slow cooker. Pour 1 inch hot water into **CROCK-POT®** slow cooker (water should not come to top of rack). Place mold on rack. Cover; cook on LOW 3½ to 4 hours or until bread pulls away from sides of mold and toothpick inserted into center comes out clean.

4. Remove mold from **CROCK-POT®** slow cooker. Let stand 10 minutes. Remove foil and run rubber spatula around outer edges, lifting bottom slightly to loosen. Invert bread onto wire rack. Let stand 10 minutes. Slice and serve with fruit and honey, if desired.

TIP: Cooking times are guidelines. **CROCK-POT®** slow cookers, just like ovens, cook differently depending on the recipe size and the individual **CROCK-POT®** slow cooker. Always check for doneness before serving.

PEAR CRUNCH

MAKES 4 SERVINGS

1 can (8 ounces) crushed pineapple in juice, undrained

¼ cup unsweetened pineapple or apple juice

3 tablespoons dried cranberries

1½ teaspoons quick-cooking tapioca

¼ teaspoon vanilla

2 pears, cored and halved

¼ cup granola with almonds

Sprigs fresh mint (optional)

1. Combine pineapple, pineapple juice, cranberries, tapioca and vanilla in **CROCK-POT**® slow cooker; stir to blend. Top with pears, cut sides down.

2. Cover; cook on LOW 3½ to 4 hours. Arrange pear halves on serving plates. Spoon pineapple mixture over pear halves. Sprinkle with granola. Garnish with mint.

WAKE-UP POTATO AND SAUSAGE BREAKFAST CASSEROLE

MAKES 8 SERVINGS

1 pound all natural nitrate-free kielbasa or smoked sausage, diced

1 cup chopped onion

1 cup chopped red bell pepper

1 package (20 ounces) refrigerated southwest-style hash browns*

10 eggs

1 cup milk

1 cup (4 ounces) shredded Monterey Jack or sharp Cheddar cheese

You may substitute O'Brien potatoes and add ½ teaspoon chile pepper.

1. Coat inside of **CROCK-POT®** slow cooker with nonstick cooking spray. Heat large skillet over medium-high heat. Add sausage and onion; cook and stir until sausage is browned. Drain fat. Stir in bell pepper.

2. Place one third of potatoes in **CROCK-POT®** slow cooker. Top with half of sausage mixture. Repeat layers. Spread remaining one third of potatoes on top.

3. Whisk eggs and milk in medium bowl. Pour evenly over potatoes. Cover; cook on LOW 6 to 7 hours.

4. Turn off heat. Sprinkle cheese over casserole; let stand 10 minutes or until cheese is melted.

TIP: To remove casserole from **CROCK-POT®** slow cooker, omit step 4. Run a rubber spatula around the edge of casserole, lifting the bottom slightly. Invert onto a large plate. Place a large serving plate on top and invert again. Sprinkle with cheese and let stand until cheese is melted. To serve, cut into wedges.

SPICED CITRUS TEA

MAKES 6 SERVINGS

4 tea bags

Peel of 1 orange

4 cups boiling water

1½ cups fresh orange juice

3 tablespoons honey

3 whole cinnamon sticks, plus additional for garnish

3 whole star anise

1. Place tea bags, orange peel and boiling water in **CROCK-POT**® slow cooker; cover and let steep 10 minutes. Remove and discard tea bags and orange peel. Add orange juice, honey, 3 cinnamon sticks and star anise.

2. Cover; cook on LOW 3 hours. Remove and discard cinnamon sticks and star anise. Garnish with additional cinnamon sticks.

BREAKFAST QUINOA

MAKES 6 SERVINGS

1½ cups uncooked quinoa

3 cups water

¼ cup maple syrup

1½ teaspoons ground cinnamon

¾ cup golden raisins

Fresh raspberries and banana slices

1. Place quinoa in fine-mesh strainer; rinse well under cold running water. Remove to **CROCK-POT**® slow cooker.

2. Stir 3 cups water, maple syrup and cinnamon into **CROCK-POT**® slow cooker. Cover; cook on LOW 5 hours or on HIGH 2½ hours or until quinoa is tender and water is absorbed.

3. Add raisins during last 10 to 15 minutes of cooking. Top quinoa with raspberries and bananas.

SPICED VANILLA APPLESAUCE

MAKES 6 CUPS

5 pounds (about 10 medium) sweet apples (such as Fuji or Gala), peeled and cut into 1-inch pieces

½ cup water

2 teaspoons vanilla

1 teaspoon ground cinnamon

¼ teaspoon ground nutmeg

¼ teaspoon ground cloves

1. Combine apples, water, vanilla, cinnamon, nutmeg and cloves in **CROCK-POT**® slow cooker; stir to blend. Cover; cook on HIGH 3 to 4 hours or until apples are very tender.

2. Turn off heat. Mash apple mixture with potato masher to smooth out any large lumps. Let cool completely before serving.

HASH BROWN AND SPINACH BREAKFAST CASSEROLE

MAKES 6 TO 8 SERVINGS

4 cups frozen southern-style diced hash browns

3 tablespoons butter

1 large onion, chopped

2 cups (8 ounces) sliced mushrooms

3 cloves garlic, minced

1 package (10 ounces) frozen chopped spinach, thawed and squeezed dry

8 eggs

1 cup milk

1 teaspoon salt

¼ teaspoon black pepper

1½ cups (6 ounces) shredded sharp Cheddar cheese, divided

1. Coat inside of **CROCK-POT**® slow cooker with nonstick cooking spray. Place hash browns in **CROCK-POT**® slow cooker.

2. Melt butter in large skillet over medium-high heat. Add onion, mushrooms and garlic; cook 4 to 5 minutes or until onion is just starting to brown, stirring occasionally. Add spinach; cook 2 minutes or until mushrooms are tender. Stir spinach mixture into **CROCK-POT**® slow cooker with hash browns until combined.

3. Combine eggs, milk, salt and pepper in large bowl; mix well. Pour over hash brown mixture in **CROCK-POT**® slow cooker. Top with 1 cup cheese. Cover; cook on LOW 4 to 4½ hours or on HIGH 1½ to 2 hours or until eggs are set. Top with remaining ½ cup cheese. Cut into wedges to serve.

HAWAIIAN FRUIT COMPOTE

MAKES 6 TO 8 SERVINGS

3 cups coarsely chopped fresh pineapple

3 grapefruits, peeled and sectioned

2½ cups pitted sweet cherries

2 cups chopped fresh peaches

2 to 3 limes, peeled and sectioned

1 mango, peeled and chopped

2 bananas, sliced

1 tablespoon fresh lemon juice

Slivered almonds (optional)

Sprigs fresh mint (optional)

Combine pineapple, grapefruits, cherries, peaches, limes, mango, bananas and lemon juice in **CROCK-POT®** slow cooker; toss to blend. Cover; cook on LOW 4 to 5 hours or on HIGH 2 to 3 hours. Sprinkle with almonds, if desired. Garnish with mint.

SERVING SUGGESTIONS: Try warm, fruity compote in place of maple syrup on your favorite waffles or pancakes for a great way to start your day.

SOUPS AND CHILIES

SIMPLE BEEF CHILI

MAKES 8 SERVINGS

- 3 pounds ground beef
- 2 cans (about 14 ounces *each*) diced tomatoes
- 2 cans (about 15 ounces *each*) kidney beans, rinsed and drained
- 2 cups chopped onions
- 1 package (10 ounces) frozen corn
- 1 cup chopped green bell pepper
- 1 can (8 ounces) tomato sauce
- 3 tablespoons chili powder
- 1 teaspoon garlic powder
- ½ teaspoon ground cumin
- ½ teaspoon dried oregano

1. Brown beef in large skillet over medium-high heat 6 to 8 minutes, stirring to break up meat. Remove to **CROCK-POT**® slow cooker using slotted spoon.

2. Add tomatoes, beans, onions, corn, bell pepper, tomato sauce, chili powder, garlic powder, cumin and oregano to **CROCK-POT**® slow cooker. Cover; cook on LOW 4 hours.

TIP: The flavor and aroma of crushed or ground herbs and spices may lessen during a longer cooking time. So, when slow cooking in your **CROCK-POT**® slow cooker, be sure to taste and adjust seasonings, if necessary, before serving.

GARLIC LENTIL SOUP WITH MUSHROOMS AND GREENS

MAKES 10 SERVINGS

¾ cup olive oil

1 whole head garlic

2 tablespoons fresh rosemary

3 medium stalks celery, diced

2 medium onions, chopped

1 bag (16 ounces) green lentils

12 fresh sage leaves

12 cups vegetable broth

1 package (8 ounces) mushrooms

8 ounces kale, spinach or Swiss chard, coarsely chopped

Chopped fresh Italian parsley (optional)

1. Place oil, garlic and rosemary in small bowl; cover with foil. Place bowl in **CROCK-POT®** slow cooker. Cover; cook on HIGH 1½ hours. Drain, reserving garlic oil and garlic cloves separately; refrigerate. Discard rosemary. (This portion of the recipe can be prepared up to 2 days in advance.)

2. Heat 2 tablespoons garlic oil in large skillet over medium-high heat. Add celery and onions; cook and stir until onions caramelize. Remove to **CROCK-POT®** slow cooker. Add lentils, sage, broth and mushrooms. Cover; cook on LOW 8 hours or on HIGH 4 hours.

3. Heat 3 to 4 tablespoons garlic oil in skillet over medium heat. Add kale; cook and stir just until tender. Stir kale into soup. Garnish with parsley, if desired.

PORK TENDERLOIN CHILI

MAKES 8 SERVINGS

1½ to 2 pounds pork tenderloin, cooked and cut into 2-inch pieces

2 cans (about 15 ounces *each*) pinto beans, rinsed and drained

2 cans (about 15 ounces *each*) black beans, rinsed and drained

2 cans (about 14 ounces *each*) whole tomatoes

2 cans (4 ounces *each*) diced mild green chiles

1 package (1¼ ounces) taco seasoning mix

Diced avocado (optional)

Combine pork, beans, tomatoes, chiles and taco seasoning mix in **CROCK-POT**® slow cooker; stir to blend. Cover; cook on LOW 4 hours. Top with avocado, if desired.

BEEF AND BEET BORSCHT

MAKES 6 TO 8 SERVINGS

- 6 slices all natural nitrate-free bacon
- 1 boneless beef chuck roast (1½ pounds), trimmed and cut into ½-inch pieces
- 1 medium onion, chopped
- 4 cloves garlic, minced
- 4 medium beets, peeled and cut into ½-inch pieces
- 2 large carrots, sliced
- 3 cups beef broth
- 6 sprigs fresh dill
- 3 tablespoons honey
- 3 tablespoons red wine vinegar
- 2 whole bay leaves
- 3 cups shredded green cabbage

1. Heat large skillet over medium heat. Add bacon; cook and stir until crisp. Remove to paper towel-lined plate using slotted spoon; crumble.

2. Return skillet to medium-high heat. Add beef; cook 5 minutes or until browned. Remove beef to **CROCK-POT®** slow cooker.

3. Pour off all but 1 tablespoon drippings from skillet. Add onion and garlic; cook 4 minutes or until onion is softened. Remove onion mixture to **CROCK-POT®** slow cooker. Stir in bacon, beets, carrots, broth, dill, honey, vinegar and bay leaves.

4. Cover; cook on LOW 5 to 6 hours. Stir in cabbage. Cover; cook on LOW 30 minutes. Remove and discard bay leaves before serving.

CHICKEN AND VEGETABLE SOUP

MAKES 10 SERVINGS

1 tablespoon olive oil

2 medium parsnips, cut into ½-inch pieces

2 medium carrots, cut into ½-inch pieces

2 medium onions, chopped

2 stalks celery, cut into ½-inch pieces

1 whole chicken (3 to 3½ pounds)

4 cups chicken broth

10 sprigs fresh Italian parsley *or* 1½ teaspoons dried parsley flakes

4 sprigs fresh thyme *or* ½ teaspoon dried thyme

1. Coat inside of **CROCK-POT**® slow cooker with nonstick cooking spray. Heat oil in large skillet over medium-high heat. Add parsnips, carrots, onions and celery; cook and stir 5 minutes or until vegetables are softened. Remove parsnip mixture to **CROCK-POT**® slow cooker. Add chicken, broth, parsley and thyme.

2. Cover; cook on LOW 6 to 7 hours. Remove chicken to large cutting board; let stand 10 minutes. Remove and discard skin and bones from chicken. Shred chicken using two forks. Stir shredded chicken back into **CROCK-POT**® slow cooker.

WHITE CHICKEN CHILI

MAKES 6 TO 8 SERVINGS

8 ounces dried navy beans, rinsed and sorted

1 tablespoon vegetable oil

2 pounds boneless, skinless chicken breasts (about 4)

2 onions, chopped

1 tablespoon minced garlic

2 teaspoons ground cumin

2 teaspoons salt

1 teaspoon dried oregano

¼ teaspoon black pepper

¼ teaspoon ground red pepper (optional)

4 cups chicken broth

1 can (4 ounces) fire-roasted diced mild green chiles, rinsed and drained

¼ cup chopped fresh cilantro

1. Place beans in bottom of **CROCK-POT®** slow cooker. Heat oil in large skillet over medium-high heat. Add chicken; cook 8 minutes or until browned on all sides. Remove to **CROCK-POT®** slow cooker.

2. Heat same skillet over medium heat. Add onions; cook 6 minutes or until softened and lightly browned. Add garlic, cumin, salt, oregano, black pepper and ground red pepper, if desired; cook and stir 1 minute. Add broth and chiles; bring to a simmer, stirring to scrape up any browned bits from bottom of skillet. Remove onion mixture to **CROCK-POT®** slow cooker.

3. Cover; cook on LOW 5 hours. Remove chicken to large cutting board; shred with two forks. Return chicken to **CROCK-POT®** slow cooker. Top each serving with cilantro.

LENTIL AND PORTOBELLO SOUP

MAKES 6 SERVINGS

- 2 portobello mushrooms (about 8 ounces)
- 1 tablespoon olive oil
- 1 medium onion, chopped
- 2 medium carrots, cut into ½-inch-thick rounds
- 2 cloves garlic, minced
- 1 cup dried lentils, rinsed and sorted
- 1 can (28 ounces) diced tomatoes
- 1 can (about 14 ounces) vegetable broth
- 1 teaspoon dried rosemary
- 1 whole bay leaf
  Salt and black pepper

1. Remove stems from mushrooms; coarsely chop stems. Cut each cap in half, then cut each half into 1-inch pieces.

2. Heat oil in large skillet over medium heat. Add onion, carrots and garlic; cook and stir 3 to 5 minutes or until onion is tender. Remove to **CROCK-POT**® slow cooker. Add mushroom caps and stems, lentils, tomatoes, broth, rosemary and bay leaf.

3. Cover; cook on HIGH 5 to 6 hours. Remove and discard bay leaf. Season with salt and pepper.

BLACK BEAN MUSHROOM CHILI

MAKES 4 SERVINGS

1 tablespoon vegetable oil

2 cups (8 ounces) sliced baby bella or button mushrooms

1 cup chopped onion

4 cloves garlic, minced

1 can (about 15 ounces) black beans, rinsed and drained

1 can (about 14 ounces) fire-roasted diced tomatoes

1 cup salsa

1 yellow or green bell pepper, finely diced

2 teaspoons chili powder or ground cumin

Sour cream (optional)

1. Coat inside of **CROCK-POT**® slow cooker with nonstick cooking spray. Heat oil in large skillet over medium heat. Add mushrooms, onion and garlic; cook 8 minutes or until mushrooms have released their liquid and liquid has thickened slightly.

2. Combine mushroom mixture, beans, tomatoes, salsa, bell pepper and chili powder in **CROCK-POT**® slow cooker; stir to blend. Cover; cook on LOW 5 to 6 hours or on HIGH 2½ to 3 hours. Ladle into shallow bowls. Top with sour cream, if desired.

CURRIED LAMB AND SWISS CHARD SOUP

MAKES 6 TO 8 SERVINGS

2 tablespoons extra virgin olive oil

1 small red onion, chopped

2 cloves garlic, minced

8 cups water

2 cups Swiss chard, trimmed, cleaned and chopped

2 cups green cabbage, cored, cleaned and chopped

2 cups cannellini beans, rinsed and sorted

2 lamb shanks

1 teaspoon salt

1 teaspoon curry powder

1 teaspoon black pepper

¼ cup fresh lemon juice

1 teaspoon grated lemon peel (optional)

Finely chopped fresh parsley (optional)

1. Heat oil in medium skillet over medium heat. Add onion and garlic; cook and stir 3 to 4 minutes or until tender. Remove to **CROCK-POT®** slow cooker.

2. Add water, Swiss chard, cabbage, beans, lamb shanks, salt, curry powder and pepper; stir to blend. Cover; cook on LOW 8 to 10 hours.

3. Remove lamb shanks to large cutting board; let stand 10 minutes. Remove and discard bones from meat. Shred lamb using two forks. Stir shredded lamb and lemon juice into **CROCK-POT®** slow cooker. Garnish each serving with lemon peel and parsley.

OLD-FASHIONED SPLIT PEA SOUP

MAKES 8 SERVINGS

- 4 quarts chicken broth
- 2 pounds dried split peas, rinsed and sorted
- 1 cup chopped cooked ham
- ½ cup chopped onion
- ½ cup chopped celery
- 2 teaspoons salt
- 2 teaspoons black pepper

Combine broth, peas, ham, onion, celery, salt and pepper in **CROCK-POT®** slow cooker; stir to blend. Cover; cook on LOW 8 to 10 hours or on HIGH 4 to 6 hours. Pour soup in batches into food processor or blender; purée until smooth.

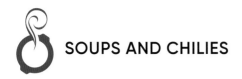

CAULIFLOWER SOUP

MAKES 8 SERVINGS

2 heads cauliflower, cut into small florets

8 cups chicken broth

¾ cup chopped celery

¾ cup chopped onion

2 teaspoons salt

2 teaspoons black pepper

2 cups milk or whipping cream

1 teaspoon Worcestershire sauce

1. Combine cauliflower, broth, celery, onion, salt and pepper in **CROCK-POT®** slow cooker. Cover; cook on LOW 7 to 8 hours or on HIGH 3 to 4 hours.

2. Pour cauliflower mixture into food processor or blender; process until smooth. Add milk and Worcestershire sauce; process until blended. Pour soup back into **CROCK-POT®** slow cooker. Cover; cook on HIGH 15 to 20 minutes or until heated through.

THREE-BEAN TURKEY CHILI

MAKES 6 TO 8 SERVINGS

- 1 pound ground turkey
- 1 small onion, chopped
- 1 can (28 ounces) diced tomatoes
- 1 can (about 15 ounces) chickpeas, rinsed and drained
- 1 can (about 15 ounces) kidney beans, rinsed and drained
- 1 can (about 15 ounces) black beans, rinsed and drained
- 1 can (8 ounces) tomato sauce
- 1 can (4 ounces) diced mild green chiles
- 1 to 2 tablespoons chili powder

1. Place turkey and onion in large skillet over medium-high heat; cook and stir 6 to 8 minutes or until turkey is browned. Remove to **CROCK-POT**® slow cooker.

2. Add tomatoes, chickpeas, beans, tomato sauce, chiles and chili powder to **CROCK-POT**® slow cooker; stir to blend. Cover; cook on HIGH 6 to 8 hours.

NORTHWEST BEEF AND VEGETABLE SOUP

MAKES 6 TO 8 SERVINGS

2 tablespoons olive oil

1 pound cubed beef stew meat

1 onion, chopped

1 clove garlic, minced

8 cups water

3½ cups canned crushed tomatoes, undrained

1 butternut squash, cut into 1-inch pieces

1 can (about 15 ounces) cannellini beans, rinsed and drained

1 turnip, peeled and cut into 1-inch pieces

1 large potato, cut into 1-inch pieces

2 stalks celery, sliced

2 tablespoons minced fresh basil

1½ teaspoons salt

1 teaspoon black pepper

1. Heat oil in large skillet over medium heat. Add beef; cook and stir 6 to 8 minutes or until browned on all sides. Add onion and garlic during last few minutes of browning. Remove to **CROCK-POT**® slow cooker.

2. Add water, tomatoes, squash, beans, turnip, potato, celery, basil, salt and pepper; stir to blend. Cover; cook on HIGH 2 hours. Turn **CROCK-POT**® slow cooker to LOW. Cover; cook on LOW 4 to 6 hours.

SAVORY CHICKEN AND OREGANO CHILI

MAKES 8 SERVINGS

3 cans (about 15 ounces *each*) cannellini beans, rinsed and drained

3½ cups chicken broth

2 cups chopped cooked chicken

2 red bell peppers, chopped

1 onion, chopped

1 can (4 ounces) diced mild green chiles, drained

3 cloves garlic, minced

2 teaspoons ground cumin

1 teaspoon salt

1 tablespoon minced fresh oregano

Place beans, broth, chicken, bell peppers, onion, chiles, garlic, cumin and salt in **CROCK-POT®** slow cooker; stir to blend. Cover; cook on LOW 8 to 10 hours or on HIGH 4 to 5 hours. Stir in oregano just before serving.

FRESH LIME AND BLACK BEAN SOUP

MAKES 4 SERVINGS

- 2 cans (about 15 ounces *each*) black beans, undrained
- 1 can (about 14 ounces) vegetable broth
- 1½ cups chopped onions
- 1½ teaspoons chili powder
- ¾ teaspoon ground cumin
- ¼ teaspoon garlic powder
- ⅛ to ¼ teaspoon red pepper flakes
- ½ cup sour cream (optional)
- 2 tablespoons extra virgin olive oil
- 2 tablespoons chopped fresh cilantro
- 1 medium lime, cut into wedges

1. Coat inside of **CROCK-POT**® slow cooker with nonstick cooking spray. Add beans, broth, onions, chili powder, cumin, garlic powder and red pepper flakes. Cover; cook on LOW 7 hours or on HIGH 3½ hours or until onions are very soft.

2. Process 1 cup soup mixture in blender until smooth and return to **CROCK-POT**® slow cooker. Stir, check consistency and repeat with additional 1 cup soup mixture as desired. Turn off heat. Let stand 15 to 20 minutes before serving.

3. Ladle soup into bowls. Divide sour cream, if desired, oil and cilantro evenly among servings. Squeeze juice from lime wedges over each.

CREAMY SWEET POTATO AND BUTTERNUT SQUASH SOUP

MAKES 4 TO 6 SERVINGS

1 pound butternut squash, cut into 1-inch cubes (about 3½ cups)

1 pound sweet potatoes, cut into 1-inch cubes (about 3 cups)

½ cup chopped onion

1 can (about 14 ounces) vegetable broth, divided

½ cup (1 stick) butter, cubed

1 can (about 13 ounces) unsweetened coconut milk

1½ teaspoons salt

½ teaspoon ground cumin

½ teaspoon ground red pepper

3 to 4 green onions, finely chopped (optional)

1. Combine squash, potatoes, onion, half of broth and butter in **CROCK-POT®** slow cooker. Cover; cook on HIGH 4 hours or until vegetables are tender.

2. Process mixture in blender, 1 cup at a time, until smooth, returning batches to **CROCK-POT®** slow cooker as they are processed. Stir in remaining broth, coconut milk, salt, cumin and ground red pepper. Cover; cook on HIGH until heated through. To serve, ladle into bowls; sprinkle with chopped green onions, if desired.

WHITE BEAN CHILI

MAKES 6 SERVINGS

1 pound ground chicken

3 cups coarsely chopped celery

1 can (28 ounces) whole tomatoes, undrained and coarsely chopped

1 can (about 15 ounces) cannellini beans, rinsed and drained

1½ cups coarsely chopped onions

1 cup chicken broth

3 cloves garlic, minced

4 teaspoons chili powder

1½ teaspoons ground cumin

¾ teaspoon ground allspice

¾ teaspoon ground cinnamon

½ teaspoon black pepper

1. Spray large skillet with nonstick cooking spray; heat over medium-high heat. Add chicken; cook 6 to 8 minutes or until browned, stirring to break up meat.

2. Combine chicken, celery, tomatoes, beans, onions, broth, garlic, chili powder, cumin, allspice, cinnamon and pepper in **CROCK-POT**® slow cooker; stir to blend. Cover; cook on LOW 5 to 6 hours.

MUSHROOM SOUP

MAKES 4 TO 6 SERVINGS

2 tablespoons olive oil

2 large Vidalia onions, coarsely chopped

1 package (10 ounces) cremini mushrooms

1 package (10 ounces) button mushrooms

Salt and black pepper

2 tablespoons butter

6 to 10 cloves garlic, peeled and coarsely chopped

2 tablespoons dry sherry

4 cups beef broth

1. Heat oil in large skillet over medium-high heat. Add onions, mushrooms, salt and pepper; cook and stir 8 to 10 minutes or until vegetables are softened.

2. Add butter and garlic; cook 1 to 2 minutes. Add sherry to skillet, scraping up any brown bits from bottom of skillet. Add vegetable mixture and broth to **CROCK-POT**® slow cooker. Cover; cook on LOW 5 to 6 hours or on HIGH 3 to 4 hours.

NOTE: Mushroom soup is usually made with beef broth, because the deep flavor of the mushrooms balances perfectly with a hearty broth. Try experimenting with a variety of mushrooms, but don't use wild mushrooms only. Although they add great flavor, they can be too intense if used exclusively.

BEEF FAJITA SOUP

MAKES 8 SERVINGS

1 pound cubed beef
  stew meat

1 can (about 15 ounces)
  pinto beans, rinsed
  and drained

1 can (about 15 ounces)
  black beans, rinsed
  and drained

1 can (about 14 ounces)
  diced tomatoes with
  roasted garlic

1 can (about 14 ounces)
  beef broth

1½ cups water

1 green bell pepper,
  thinly sliced

1 red bell pepper, thinly
  sliced

1 onion, thinly sliced

2 teaspoons ground
  cumin

1 teaspoon seasoned
  salt

1 teaspoon black
  pepper

Optional toppings:
  sour cream,
  shredded cheese
  and/or chopped
  olives

Combine beef, beans, tomatoes, broth, water, bell peppers, onion, cumin, salt and black pepper in **CROCK-POT**® slow cooker; stir to blend. Cover; cook on LOW 8 hours. Top as desired.

VEGETARIAN

HEARTY VEGETARIAN MAC AND CHEESE

MAKES 6 SERVINGS

1 can (about 14 ounces) stewed tomatoes, undrained

1½ cups prepared Alfredo sauce

1½ cups (6 ounces) shredded mozzarella cheese, divided

8 ounces whole grain pasta, cooked and drained

7 ounces all natural nitrate-free, Italian-flavored vegetarian sausage links, ¼-inch slices

¾ cup fresh basil leaves, thinly sliced and divided

½ cup vegetable broth

½ teaspoon salt

2 tablespoons grated Parmesan cheese

1. Coat inside of **CROCK-POT®** slow cooker with nonstick cooking spray. Add tomatoes, Alfredo sauce, 1 cup mozzarella cheese, pasta, sausage, ½ cup basil, broth and salt to **CROCK-POT®** slow cooker; stir to blend. Top with remaining ½ cup mozzarella cheese and Parmesan cheese.

2. Cover; cook on LOW 3½ hours or on HIGH 2 hours. Top with remaining ¼ cup basil.

SOUTHWESTERN STUFFED PEPPERS

MAKES 4 SERVINGS

4 green bell peppers

1 can (about 15 ounces) black beans, rinsed and drained

1 cup (4 ounces) shredded pepper jack cheese

¾ cup salsa

½ cup frozen corn, thawed

½ cup chopped green onions

⅓ cup uncooked brown rice

1 teaspoon chili powder

½ teaspoon ground cumin

Sour cream (optional)

1. Cut thin slice off top of each bell pepper. Carefully remove seeds and membranes, leaving bell peppers whole.

2. Combine beans, cheese, salsa, corn, green onions, rice, chili powder and cumin in medium bowl. Spoon bean mixture evenly into each bell pepper. Place bell peppers in **CROCK-POT®** slow cooker.

3. Cover; cook on LOW 4 to 6 hours. Serve with sour cream, if desired.

HEARTY LENTIL STEW

MAKES 6 SERVINGS

1 cup dried lentils,
   rinsed and sorted

1 package (16 ounces)
   frozen green beans

2 cups cauliflower
   florets

1 cup chopped onion

1 cup baby carrots, cut
   into halves crosswise

3 cups vegetable broth

2 teaspoons ground
   cumin

¾ teaspoon ground
   ginger

1 can (15 ounces)
   chunky tomato sauce
   with garlic and herbs

½ cup peanuts

1. Layer lentils, beans, cauliflower, onion and carrots in **CROCK-POT**® slow cooker. Combine broth, cumin and ginger in large bowl; stir to blend. Pour over vegetables in **CROCK-POT**® slow cooker.

2. Cover; cook on LOW 9 to 11 hours. Stir in tomato sauce. Cover; cook on LOW 10 minutes or until heated through. Sprinkle each serving evenly with peanuts.

BARLEY WITH CURRANTS AND PINE NUTS

MAKES 4 SERVINGS

1 tablespoon butter

1 small onion, finely chopped

2 cups vegetable broth

½ cup uncooked pearl barley

½ teaspoon salt

¼ teaspoon black pepper

⅓ cup currants

¼ cup pine nuts

Sprigs fresh sage (optional)

Melt butter in small skillet over medium-high heat. Add onion; cook and stir 2 minutes or until lightly browned. Remove to **CROCK-POT**® slow cooker. Add broth, barley, salt and pepper to **CROCK-POT**® slow cooker. Stir in currants. Cover; cook on LOW 3 hours. Stir in pine nuts just before serving. Garnish with sage.

CARIBBEAN SWEET POTATO AND BEAN STEW

MAKES 4 SERVINGS

2 medium sweet potatoes (about 1 pound), cut into 1-inch cubes

2 cups frozen cut green beans

1 can (about 15 ounces) black beans, rinsed and drained

1 can (about 14 ounces) vegetable broth

1 small onion, sliced

2 teaspoons Caribbean jerk seasoning

½ teaspoon dried thyme

¼ teaspoon salt

¼ teaspoon ground cinnamon

⅓ cup slivered almonds, toasted*

*To toast almonds, spread in single layer in heavy skillet. Cook and stir over medium heat 1 to 2 minutes or until nuts are lightly browned.

Combine potatoes, beans, broth, onion, jerk seasoning, thyme, salt and cinnamon in **CROCK-POT**® slow cooker. Cover; cook on LOW 5 to 6 hours. Sprinkle each serving evenly with almonds.

BARLEY AND VEGETABLE RISOTTO

MAKES 6 SERVINGS

2 teaspoons olive oil

1 small onion, diced

8 ounces sliced mushrooms

¾ cup uncooked pearl barley

1 large red bell pepper, diced

4½ cups vegetable broth

2 cups packed baby spinach

¼ cup grated Parmesan cheese

¼ teaspoon black pepper

1. Heat oil in large skillet over medium-high heat. Add onion; cook and stir 2 minutes or until lightly browned. Add mushrooms; cook and stir 5 minutes or until mushrooms have released their liquid and are just beginning to brown. Remove to **CROCK-POT®** slow cooker.

2. Add barley and bell pepper to **CROCK-POT®** slow cooker; pour in broth. Cover; cook on LOW 4 to 5 hours or on HIGH 2½ to 3 hours or until barley is tender and liquid is absorbed.

3. Stir in spinach. Turn off heat. Let stand 5 minutes. Gently stir in cheese and black pepper just before serving.

CHUNKY ITALIAN STEW WITH WHITE BEANS

MAKES 8 SERVINGS

2 teaspoons olive oil

4 green bell peppers, cut into ¾-inch pieces

2 yellow squash, cut into ¾-inch pieces

2 zucchini, cut into ¾-inch pieces

2 onions, cut into ¾-inch pieces

8 ounces mushrooms, quartered (about 2 cups)

2 cans (about 15 ounces *each*) navy beans, rinsed and drained

2 cans (about 14 ounces *each*) diced tomatoes

2 teaspoons dried oregano

1 teaspoon Italian seasoning

¼ teaspoon red pepper flakes (optional)

1½ cups (6 ounces) shredded mozzarella cheese

2 tablespoons grated Parmesan cheese

1. Heat oil in large nonstick skillet over medium-high heat. Add bell peppers, squash, zucchini, onions and mushrooms; cook and stir 8 minutes or until onions are translucent. Remove to **CROCK-POT**® slow cooker.

2. Add beans, tomatoes, oregano, Italian seasoning and red pepper flakes, if desired, to **CROCK-POT**® slow cooker; stir to blend. Cover; cook on LOW 7 to 8 hours. Top with cheeses just before serving.

RATATOUILLE WITH PARMESAN CHEESE

MAKES 4 SERVINGS

- 1 cup diced eggplant
- 2 medium tomatoes, chopped
- 1 small zucchini, diced
- 1 cup sliced mushrooms
- ½ cup tomato purée
- 1 large shallot *or* ½ small onion, chopped
- 1 clove garlic, minced
- ¾ teaspoon dried oregano
- ⅛ teaspoon dried rosemary
- ⅛ teaspoon black pepper
- 2 tablespoons shredded fresh basil
- 2 teaspoons fresh lemon juice
- ¼ teaspoon salt
- Grated Parmesan cheese

1. Spray large skillet with nonstick cooking spray; heat over medium-high heat. Add eggplant; cook and stir 5 minutes or until lightly browned. Remove eggplant to **CROCK-POT**® slow cooker.

2. Add tomatoes, zucchini, mushrooms, tomato purée, shallot, garlic, oregano, rosemary and pepper; stir to blend. Cover; cook on LOW 6 hours or on HIGH 3 hours.

3. Stir in basil, lemon juice and salt. Turn off heat; let stand 5 minutes. Top each serving with Parmesan cheese.

ITALIAN ESCAROLE AND WHITE BEAN STEW

MAKES 4 SERVINGS

- 1 tablespoon olive oil
- 1 medium onion, chopped
- 3 medium carrots, cut into ½-inch-thick rounds
- 2 cloves garlic, minced
- 1 can (about 14 ounces) vegetable broth
- 1 head (about 12 ounces) escarole, base trimmed
- ¼ teaspoon red pepper flakes
- 2 cans (about 15 ounces *each*) cannellini beans, rinsed and drained

  Grated Parmesan cheese (optional)

1. Heat oil in medium skillet over medium-high heat. Add onion and carrots; cook and stir 3 to 5 minutes or until onion is softened. Add garlic; cook and stir 1 minute or until fragrant. Remove to **CROCK-POT**® slow cooker. Top with broth.

2. Roughly cut escarole crosswise into 1-inch-wide strips. Wash well in large bowl of cold water. Shake to remove excess water, leaving dirt in bottom of bowl. Add to vegetable mixture in **CROCK-POT**® slow cooker. Sprinkle with red pepper flakes. Top with beans.

3. Cover; cook on LOW 7 to 8 hours or on HIGH 3½ to 4 hours. Garnish with cheese.

TIP: Escarole is very leafy and easily fills a 4½-quart **CROCK-POT**® slow cooker when raw, but it shrinks dramatically as it cooks down. This recipe makes four servings, but can easily be doubled. Simply double the quantities of all the ingredients listed and be sure to use a 6-quart (or larger) **CROCK-POT**® slow cooker.

ASIAN KALE AND CHICKPEAS

MAKES 4 SERVINGS

1 tablespoon sesame oil

1 medium onion, thinly sliced

2 teaspoons grated fresh ginger

2 cloves garlic, minced

2 jalapeño peppers, chopped*

8 cups chopped kale

1 cup vegetable broth

2 cans (about 15 ounces *each*) chickpeas, rinsed and drained

1 tablespoon lime juice

1 teaspoon grated lime peel

2 cups hot cooked brown rice (optional)

Jalapeño peppers can sting and irritate the skin, so wear rubber gloves when handling peppers and do not touch your eyes.

1. Coat inside of **CROCK-POT**® slow cooker with nonstick cooking spray. Heat oil in large skillet over medium-high heat. Add onion, ginger, garlic and jalapeño peppers; cook 1 minute. Add kale; cook and stir 2 minutes or until slightly wilted. Remove kale mixture to **CROCK-POT**® slow cooker. Add broth and chickpeas.

2. Cover; cook on LOW 3 hours. Turn off heat. Stir in lime juice and lime peel. Serve with rice, if desired.

BUTTERNUT SQUASH, CHICKPEA AND LENTIL STEW

MAKES 6 SERVINGS

2 cups peeled and diced butternut squash (½-inch pieces)

2 cups vegetable broth

1 can (about 15 ounces) chickpeas, rinsed and drained

1 can (about 14 ounces) fire-roasted diced tomatoes

1 cup chopped sweet onion

¾ cup dried brown lentils, rinsed and sorted

2 teaspoons ground cumin or coriander *or* 1 teaspoon *each*)

¾ teaspoon salt

Olive oil (optional)

Sprigs fresh thyme (optional)

Coat inside of **CROCK-POT®** slow cooker with nonstick cooking spray. Combine squash, broth, chickpeas, tomatoes, onion, lentils, cumin and salt in **CROCK-POT®** slow cooker. Cover; cook on LOW 8 to 9 hours or on HIGH 4 to 4½ hours or until squash and lentils are tender. Ladle into shallow bowls. Drizzle with oil, if desired. Garnish with thyme.

BLACK BEAN STUFFED PEPPERS

MAKES 6 SERVINGS

1 medium onion, finely chopped

¼ teaspoon ground red pepper

¼ teaspoon dried oregano

¼ teaspoon ground cumin

¼ teaspoon chili powder

1 can (about 15 ounces) black beans, rinsed and drained

6 large green bell peppers, tops removed

1 cup (4 ounces) shredded Monterey Jack cheese

1 cup tomato salsa

½ cup sour cream (optional)

1. Spray medium skillet with nonstick cooking spray; heat over medium heat. Add onion; cook and stir 3 to 5 minutes or until golden. Add ground red pepper, oregano, cumin and chili powder; cook and stir 1 minute.

2. Mash half of beans with onion mixture in medium bowl; stir in remaining half of beans. Spoon black bean mixture into bell peppers; sprinkle with cheese. Pour salsa over cheese. Place bell peppers in **CROCK-POT**® slow cooker.

3. Cover; cook on LOW 6 to 8 hours or on HIGH 3 to 4 hours. Serve with sour cream, if desired.

TIP: You may increase any of the recipe ingredients to taste except the tomato salsa.

SPINACH ARTICHOKE GRATIN

MAKES 6 SERVINGS

2 cups (16 ounces) cottage cheese

2 eggs

4½ tablespoons grated Parmesan cheese, divided

1 tablespoon fresh lemon juice

⅛ teaspoon ground nutmeg

⅛ teaspoon black pepper

2 packages (10 ounces *each*) frozen chopped spinach, thawed and squeezed dry

⅓ cup thinly sliced green onions

1 package (10 ounces) frozen artichoke hearts, thawed and halved

1. Add cottage cheese, eggs, 3 tablespoons Parmesan cheese, lemon juice, nutmeg and pepper to food processor or blender; process until smooth.

2. Coat inside of **CROCK-POT**® slow cooker with nonstick cooking spray. Combine cottage cheese mixture, spinach and green onions in large bowl. Spread half of mixture in **CROCK-POT**® slow cooker.

3. Pat artichoke halves dry with paper towels; place in single layer over spinach mixture. Top with remaining spinach mixture. Cover with lid slightly ajar to allow excess moisture to escape. Cover; cook on LOW 3 to 3½ hours or on HIGH 2 to 2½ hours. Sprinkle with remaining 1½ tablespoons Parmesan cheese before serving.

JAMAICAN QUINOA AND SWEET POTATO STEW

MAKES 4 SERVINGS

3 cups vegetable broth

1 large *or* 2 small sweet potatoes (12 ounces), cut into ¾-inch pieces

1 cup uncooked quinoa, rinsed and drained

1 large red bell pepper, cut into ¾-inch pieces

1 tablespoon Caribbean jerk seasoning

¼ cup chopped fresh cilantro

¼ cup sliced almonds, toasted*

Hot pepper sauce or Pickapeppa sauce (optional)

To toast almonds, spread in single layer in heavy skillet. Cook and stir over medium heat 1 to 2 minutes or until nuts are lightly browned.

1. Coat inside of **CROCK-POT**® slow cooker with nonstick cooking spray. Combine broth, potatoes, quinoa, bell pepper and jerk seasoning in **CROCK-POT**® slow cooker; stir to blend.

2. Cover; cook on LOW 5 to 6 hours or on HIGH 2 to 2½ hours. Top each serving with cilantro and almonds. Serve with hot pepper sauce, if desired.

SUMMER VEGETABLE STEW

MAKES 4 SERVINGS

1 cup vegetable broth

1 can (about 15 ounces) chickpeas, rinsed and drained

1 medium zucchini, cut into ½-inch pieces

1 summer squash, cut into ½-inch pieces

4 large plum tomatoes, cut into ½-inch pieces

1 cup frozen corn

½ to 1 teaspoon dried rosemary

¼ cup grated Asiago or Parmesan cheese

1 tablespoon chopped fresh Italian parsley

Combine broth, chickpeas, zucchini, squash, tomatoes, corn and rosemary in **CROCK-POT**® slow cooker; stir to blend. Cover; cook on LOW 8 hours or on HIGH 5 hours. Top each serving evenly with cheese and parsley.

TIP: Layer the ingredients in the order given in this recipe to ensure they will cook properly.

QUINOA AND VEGETABLE MEDLEY

MAKES 6 SERVINGS

2 medium sweet
   potatoes, cut into
   ½-inch-thick slices

1 medium eggplant, cut
   into ½-inch cubes

1 large green bell
   pepper, sliced

1 medium tomato, cut
   into wedges

1 small onion, cut into
   wedges

½ teaspoon salt

¼ teaspoon ground red
   pepper

¼ teaspoon black
   pepper

1 cup uncooked quinoa

2 cups vegetable broth

2 cloves garlic, minced

½ teaspoon dried thyme

¼ teaspoon dried
   marjoram

1. Coat inside of **CROCK-POT®** slow cooker with nonstick cooking spray. Combine potatoes, eggplant, bell pepper, tomato, onion, salt, ground red pepper and black pepper in **CROCK-POT®** slow cooker; toss to coat.

2. Place quinoa in strainer; rinse well. Add quinoa to vegetable mixture in **CROCK-POT®** slow cooker. Stir in broth, garlic, thyme and marjoram. Cover; cook on LOW 5 hours or on HIGH 2½ hours or until broth is absorbed.

MUSHROOM BARLEY STEW

MAKES 8 SERVINGS

2 containers (32 ounces *each*) vegetable broth

1 package (8 ounces) mushrooms, such as cremini, rinsed and thinly sliced

1 cup dried mushrooms, porcini if possible, soaked in warm water to cover to soften, liquid reserved

1 cup uncooked pearl barley, rinsed and sorted (about ½ pound)

2 carrots, diced

2 stalks celery, diced

1 yellow onion, diced

1 tablespoon fresh thyme

1 tablespoon tomato paste

2 whole bay leaves

Salt and black pepper

2 tablespoons minced fresh Italian parsley (optional)

1. Combine broth, mushrooms, reserved mushroom liquid (taking care to discard any grit), barley, carrots, celery, onion, thyme, tomato paste, bay leaves, salt and black pepper in **CROCK-POT®** slow cooker.

2. Cover; cook on LOW 5½ hours or on HIGH 3 to 4 hours or until barley and vegetables are tender. Add additional warm broth if needed during cooking. Remove and discard bay leaves. Garnish with parsley.

THAI RED CURRY WITH TOFU

MAKES 4 SERVINGS

1 medium sweet potato, cut into 1-inch pieces

1 small eggplant, halved lengthwise and cut crosswise into ½-inch-wide halves

8 ounces extra firm tofu, cut into 1-inch pieces

½ cup green beans, cut into 1-inch pieces

½ red bell pepper, cut into ¼-inch-wide strips

2 tablespoons vegetable oil

5 medium shallots (about 1½ cups), thinly sliced

3 tablespoons Thai red curry paste

1 teaspoon minced garlic

1 teaspoon grated ginger

1 can (about 13 ounces) unsweetened coconut milk

1½ tablespoons soy sauce

¼ cup chopped fresh basil

2 tablespoons lime juice

Hot cooked brown rice (optional)

1. Coat inside of **CROCK-POT**® slow cooker with nonstick cooking spray. Add potato, eggplant, tofu, beans and bell pepper.

2. Heat oil in large skillet over medium heat. Add shallots; cook 5 minutes or until browned and tender. Add curry paste, garlic and ginger; cook and stir 1 minute. Add coconut milk and soy sauce; bring to a simmer. Pour mixture over vegetables in **CROCK-POT**® slow cooker.

3. Cover; cook on LOW 2 to 3 hours. Stir in basil and lime juice. Serve with rice, if desired.

STEAMED ARTICHOKES WITH THREE SAUCES

MAKES 8 SERVINGS

4 artichokes, trimmed and cut in half

Juice of ½ lemon

Dipping Sauces (recipes follow)

Place trimmed artichokes cut side down in bottom of **CROCK-POT**® slow cooker. Add enough water to come halfway up artichokes; add lemon juice. Cover; cook on LOW 6 hours. Serve with one or more Dipping Sauces.

TARRAGON BROWNED BUTTER DIPPING SAUCE

MAKES ABOUT 1 CUP

1 cup (2 sticks) butter

4 teaspoons dried tarragon *or* ¼ cup finely chopped fresh tarragon

Melt butter in medium saucepan over medium heat. Cook, swirling butter in saucepan over heat until butter is light brown. Remove from heat and stir in tarragon. Cover to keep warm.

CREAM CHEESE DIPPING SAUCE

MAKES ABOUT 1 CUP

4 ounces cream cheese

1 cup whipping cream

½ teaspoon black pepper

8 slices all natural nitrate-free vegetarian bacon, crisp-cooked and finely chopped

Whisk cream cheese and cream in medium saucepan over medium heat until smooth. Stir in pepper and bacon. Cover to keep warm.

GARLIC-HERB BUTTER DIPPING SAUCE

MAKES ABOUT 1 CUP

1 cup (2 sticks) butter

8 cloves garlic, crushed

½ cup chopped fresh herbs such as Italian parsley, tarragon and chives

Melt butter in medium saucepan over medium heat. Add garlic; cook and stir until garlic is golden brown. Remove from heat. Strain garlic from sauce; stir in herbs. Cover to keep warm.

MAIN DISHES

CHICKEN AND BUTTERNUT SQUASH

MAKES 6 SERVINGS

6 boneless, skinless chicken thighs (1½ pounds)

1 (1½- to 2-pound) butternut squash, cubed

2 tablespoons balsamic vinegar

4 cloves garlic, minced

6 fresh sage leaves

Salt and black pepper

Place chicken, squash, vinegar, garlic, sage, salt and pepper in **CROCK-POT®** slow cooker. Cover; cook on LOW 4 to 6 hours.

ITALIAN-STYLE POT ROAST

MAKES 6 TO 8 SERVINGS

2 teaspoons minced garlic

1 teaspoon salt

1 teaspoon dried basil

1 teaspoon dried oregano

¼ teaspoon red pepper flakes

1 boneless beef bottom round rump roast or chuck shoulder roast (about 2½ to 3 pounds)*

1 large onion, quartered and thinly sliced

1½ cups tomato-basil or marinara pasta sauce

2 cans (about 15 ounces *each*) cannellini or Great Northern beans, rinsed and drained

¼ cup shredded fresh basil (optional)

*Unless you have a 5-, 6- or 7-quart **CROCK-POT**® slow cooker, cut any roast larger than 2½ pounds in half so it cooks completely.*

1. Combine garlic, salt, dried basil, oregano and red pepper flakes in small bowl; rub over roast.

2. Place onion slices in **CROCK-POT**® slow cooker. Place roast over onion slices in **CROCK-POT**® slow cooker. Pour pasta sauce over roast. Cover; cook on LOW 8 to 9 hours or until roast is fork-tender.

3. Remove roast to large cutting board. Cover loosely with foil; let stand 10 to 15 minutes. Turn off heat. Let liquid in **CROCK-POT**® slow cooker stand 5 minutes to allow fat to rise. Skim off and discard fat.

4. Stir beans into liquid. Cover; cook on LOW 15 to 30 minutes or until beans are heated through. Slice roast across the grain into thin slices. Serve with bean mixture. Garnish with fresh basil.

BONELESS PORK ROAST WITH GARLIC

MAKES 4 TO 6 SERVINGS

1 boneless pork
   rib roast (2 to
   2½ pounds)

   Salt and black pepper

3 tablespoons olive oil,
   divided

4 cloves garlic, minced

¼ cup chopped fresh
   rosemary

½ lemon, cut into ⅛- to
   ¼-inch slices

½ cup chicken broth

¼ cup dry white wine

1. Season pork with salt and pepper. Combine 2 tablespoons oil, garlic and rosemary in small bowl. Rub over pork. Roll and tie pork with kitchen string. Tuck lemon slices under string and into ends of roast.

2. Heat remaining 1 tablespoon oil in skillet over medium heat. Add pork; cook 6 to 8 minutes or until browned on all sides. Remove to **CROCK-POT**® slow cooker.

3. Return skillet to heat. Add broth and wine, scraping up any browned bits from bottom of skillet. Pour over pork in **CROCK-POT**® slow cooker. Cover; cook on LOW 8 to 9 hours or on HIGH 3½ to 4 hours.

4. Remove roast to large cutting board. Cover loosely with foil; let stand 10 to 15 minutes before removing kitchen string and slicing. Pour pan juices over sliced pork to serve.

JAMAICA-ME-CRAZY CHICKEN TROPICALE

MAKES 4 SERVINGS

2 sweet potatoes, cut into 2-inch pieces

1 can (20 ounces) pineapple tidbits in pineapple juice, drained and juice reserved

1 can (8 ounces) water chestnuts, drained and sliced

1 cup golden raisins

4 boneless, skinless chicken breasts

4 teaspoons Caribbean jerk seasoning

¼ cup dried onion flakes

3 tablespoons grated fresh ginger

2 tablespoons Worcestershire sauce

1 tablespoon grated lime peel

1 teaspoon whole cumin seeds, slightly crushed

Hot cooked brown rice (optional)

1. Place potatoes in **CROCK-POT**® slow cooker. Add pineapple, water chestnuts and raisins; toss well.

2. Sprinkle chicken with seasoning. Place chicken on top of sweet potato mixture.

3. Combine reserved pineapple juice, onion flakes, ginger, Worcestershire sauce, lime peel and cumin seeds in small bowl; pour over chicken. Cover; cook on LOW 7 to 9 hours or on HIGH 3 to 4 hours or until chicken and potatoes are fork-tender. Serve with rice, if desired.

TURKEY BREAST WITH BARLEY-CRANBERRY STUFFING

MAKES 6 SERVINGS

2 cups chicken broth

1 cup uncooked quick-cooking barley

½ cup chopped onion

½ cup dried cranberries

2 tablespoons slivered almonds, toasted*

½ teaspoon rubbed sage

½ teaspoon garlic-pepper seasoning

1 fresh or thawed frozen bone-in turkey breast half (about 2 pounds), skinned

⅓ cup finely chopped fresh Italian parsley

To toast almonds, spread in single layer in heavy skillet. Cook over medium heat 1 to 2 minutes or until nuts are lightly browned, stirring frequently.

1. Combine broth, barley, onion, cranberries, almonds, sage and garlic-pepper seasoning in **CROCK-POT**® slow cooker.

2. Coat large skillet with nonstick cooking spray; heat over medium heat. Brown turkey breast on all sides; add to **CROCK-POT**® slow cooker. Cover; cook on LOW 4 to 6 hours.

3. Remove turkey to large cutting board; cover loosely with foil. Let stand 10 to 15 minutes before slicing. Stir parsley into stuffing in **CROCK-POT**® slow cooker. Serve with turkey.

TIP: Browning poultry before cooking it in the **CROCK-POT**® slow cooker isn't necessary but helps to enhance the flavor and adds color.

THAI STEAK SALAD

MAKES 4 TO 6 SERVINGS

¼ cup soy sauce

5 cloves garlic, minced and divided

3 tablespoons honey

1 pound boneless beef chuck steak, about ¾ inch thick

¼ cup hoisin sauce

2 tablespoons creamy peanut butter

½ cup water

1 tablespoon minced fresh ginger

1 tablespoon ketchup or tomato paste

2 teaspoons lime juice

¼ teaspoon hot chili sauce or sriracha

½ head savoy cabbage, shredded

1 bag (10 ounces) romaine lettuce with carrots and red cabbage

1 cup fresh cilantro leaves

¾ cup chopped mango

½ cup chopped peanuts

Fresh lime wedges

1. Coat inside of **CROCK-POT**® slow cooker with nonstick cooking spray. Combine soy sauce, 3 cloves minced garlic and honey in **CROCK-POT**® slow cooker; stir to blend. Add steak; turn to coat. Cover; cook on HIGH 3 hours.

2. Remove steak to large cutting board. Cover loosely with foil; let stand 10 to 15 minutes. Slice against the grain into ¼-inch strips. Cover with plastic wrap and refrigerate until needed.

3. Combine hoisin sauce and peanut butter in medium bowl; stir until smooth. Add water, remaining 2 cloves minced garlic, ginger, ketchup, lime juice and chili sauce; stir until well blended. Toss cabbage and romaine salad mix with hoisin dressing in large salad bowl. Top with reserved steak. Sprinkle with cilantro, mango and peanuts. Serve with lime wedges.

TIP: The **CROCK-POT**® slow cooker cooks at a low heat for a long time, so it is perfect for dishes calling for less-tender cuts of meat.

BRISKET WITH SWEET ONIONS

MAKES 10 SERVINGS

2 large sweet onions, cut into 10 (½-inch) slices*

1 flat-cut boneless beef brisket (about 3½ pounds)**

Salt and black pepper

2 cans (about 14 ounces *each*) beef broth

1 teaspoon cracked black peppercorns

¾ cup crumbled blue cheese (optional)

Preferably Maui, Vidalia or Walla Walla onions.

Unless you have a 5-, 6- or 7-quart **CROCK-POT® slow cooker, cut any piece of meat larger than 2½ pounds in half so it cooks completely.*

1. Coat inside of **CROCK-POT**® slow cooker with nonstick cooking spray. Line bottom with onion slices.

2. Season brisket with salt and black pepper. Heat large skillet over medium-high heat. Add brisket; cook 10 to 12 minutes or until browned on all sides. Remove to **CROCK-POT**® slow cooker.

3. Pour broth into **CROCK-POT**® slow cooker. Sprinkle brisket with peppercorns. Cover; cook on HIGH 5 to 7 hours.

4. Remove brisket to large cutting board. Cover loosely with foil; let stand 10 to 15 minutes. Slice evenly against the grain into ten slices. To serve, arrange onions on serving platter and spread slices of brisket on top. Sprinkle with blue cheese, if desired. Serve with cooking liquid.

BRAISED SEA BASS WITH AROMATIC VEGETABLES

MAKES 6 SERVINGS

2 tablespoons butter or olive oil

2 fennel bulbs, thinly sliced

3 large carrots, julienned

3 large leeks, cleaned and thinly sliced

Salt and black pepper

6 sea bass fillets or other firm-fleshed white fish (2 to 3 pounds)

1. Melt butter in large skillet over medium-high heat. Add fennel, carrots and leeks; cook and stir 6 to 8 minutes or until beginning to soften and lightly brown. Season with salt and pepper. Arrange half of vegetables in bottom of **CROCK-POT**® slow cooker.

2. Season bass with salt and pepper; place on top of vegetables in **CROCK-POT**® slow cooker. Top with remaining vegetables. Cover; cook on LOW 2 to 3 hours or on HIGH 1 to 1½ hours.

BASQUE CHICKEN WITH PEPPERS

MAKES 4 TO 6 SERVINGS

1 cut-up whole chicken (about 4 pounds)

2 teaspoons salt, divided

1 teaspoon black pepper, divided

1½ tablespoons olive oil

1 onion, chopped

1 medium green bell pepper, cut into strips

1 medium yellow bell pepper, cut into strips

1 medium red bell pepper, cut into strips

8 ounces small brown mushrooms, halved

1 can (about 14 ounces) stewed tomatoes

½ cup chicken broth

½ cup Rioja wine

3 ounces tomato paste

2 cloves garlic, minced

1 sprig fresh marjoram

1 teaspoon smoked paprika

1. Season chicken with 1 teaspoon salt and ½ teaspoon black pepper. Heat oil in large skillet over medium-high heat. Add chicken in batches; cook 6 to 8 minutes or until browned on all sides. Remove to **CROCK-POT®** slow cooker.

2. Heat same skillet over medium-low heat. Add onion; cook and stir 3 minutes or until softened. Add bell peppers and mushrooms; cook 3 minutes. Add tomatoes, broth, wine, tomato paste, garlic, marjoram, remaining 1 teaspoon salt, paprika and remaining ½ teaspoon black pepper to skillet; bring to a simmer. Simmer 3 to 4 minutes; pour over chicken in **CROCK-POT®** slow cooker.

3. Cover; cook on LOW 5 to 6 hours or on HIGH 3 to 4 hours. Ladle vegetables and sauce over chicken.

SPICY TURKEY WITH CITRUS AU JUS

MAKES 6 TO 8 SERVINGS

1 bone-in turkey breast, rinsed and patted dry (about 4 pounds)

¼ cup (½ stick) butter, softened

Grated peel of 1 medium lemon

1 teaspoon chili powder

¼ teaspoon black pepper, plus additional for seasoning

⅛ to ¼ teaspoon red pepper flakes

1 tablespoon fresh lemon juice

Salt

1. Coat inside of **CROCK-POT®** slow cooker with nonstick cooking spray. Add turkey breast.

2. Mix butter, lemon peel, chili powder, ¼ teaspoon black pepper and red pepper flakes in small bowl until well blended. Spread mixture over top and sides of turkey. Cover; cook on LOW 4 to 5 hours or on HIGH 2½ to 3 hours.

3. Turn off heat. Remove turkey to large cutting board. Cover loosely with foil; let stand 10 to 15 minutes before slicing.

4. Let cooking liquid stand 5 minutes. Skim off and discard fat. Stir lemon juice into cooking liquid. Season with salt and additional black pepper. Serve turkey with sauce.

BRAISED CHIPOTLE BEEF

MAKES 4 TO 6 SERVINGS

- 3 pounds boneless beef chuck roast, cut into 2-inch pieces
- 1½ teaspoons salt, plus additional for seasoning
- ½ teaspoon black pepper, plus additional for seasoning
- 3 tablespoons vegetable oil, divided
- 1 large onion, cut into 1-inch pieces
- 2 red bell peppers, cut into 1-inch pieces
- 3 tablespoons tomato paste
- 1 tablespoon minced garlic
- 1 tablespoon chipotle chili powder*
- 1 tablespoon paprika
- 1 tablespoon ground cumin
- 1 teaspoon dried oregano
- 1 cup beef broth
- 1 can (about 14 ounces) diced tomatoes, drained

Or substitute conventional chili powder.

1. Season beef with salt and black pepper. Heat 2 tablespoons oil in large skillet over medium-high heat. Add beef in batches; cook 5 to 7 minutes or until browned on all sides. Remove each batch to **CROCK-POT®** slow cooker using slotted spoon.

2. Return skillet to medium-high heat. Add remaining 1 tablespoon oil. Add onion; cook and stir just until softened. Add bell peppers; cook 2 minutes. Stir in tomato paste, garlic, chili powder, paprika, cumin, 1½ teaspoons salt, oregano and ½ teaspoon black pepper; cook and stir 1 minute. Remove to **CROCK-POT®** slow cooker.

3. Return skillet to medium heat. Add broth; cook, stirring to scrape up any browned bits from bottom of skillet. Pour over beef in **CROCK-POT®** slow cooker; stir in tomatoes. Cover; cook on LOW 7 hours. Turn off heat. Let cooking liquid stand 5 minutes. Skim off and discard fat. Serve beef with cooking liquid.

ASIAN PORK TENDERLOIN

MAKES 4 SERVINGS

½ cup bottled garlic ginger sauce

¼ cup sliced green onions

1 pork tenderloin (about 1 pound)

1 large red onion, cut into slices

1 medium red bell pepper, cut into 1-inch pieces

1 medium zucchini, cut into ¼-inch slices

1 tablespoon olive oil

1. Combine sauce and green onions in large resealable food storage bag. Add pork. Seal bag; turn to coat. Place bag in large baking pan; refrigerate 30 minutes or overnight.

2. Combine red onion, bell pepper, zucchini and oil in large bowl; toss to coat. Place vegetables in **CROCK-POT**® slow cooker. Remove pork from bag; place on top of vegetables. Discard marinade. Cover; cook on LOW 6 to 7 hours or on HIGH 4 to 5 hours.

3. Remove pork to large cutting board. Cover loosely with foil; let stand 10 to 15 minutes before slicing. Serve pork with vegetables.

SIMPLE SALMON WITH FRESH SALSA

MAKES 4 SERVINGS

- 4 salmon fillets (about 4 ounces *each*), rinsed and patted dry
- 1 teaspoon salt, divided
- ½ teaspoon dried thyme, crumbled
- ¼ teaspoon black pepper
- ½ cup chicken broth
- 1 medium cucumber, peeled, seeded and chopped
- ½ large green bell pepper, chopped
- ½ cup finely chopped radishes
- ½ cup quartered grape tomatoes
- ¼ cup chopped fresh cilantro
- 3 tablespoons fresh lime juice
- 2 tablespoons finely chopped red onion
- Hot cooked green beans (optional)

1. Season salmon with ½ teaspoon salt, thyme and black pepper. Pour broth into **CROCK-POT®** slow cooker; add salmon. Cover; cook on LOW 3 hours.

2. Meanwhile, combine cucumber, bell pepper, radishes, tomatoes, cilantro, lime juice, onion and remaining ½ teaspoon salt in medium bowl. Cover; refrigerate until ready to serve.

3. To serve, place salmon on serving plates; top with salsa. Serve with green beans, if desired.

BRAISED BEEF BRISKET

MAKES 6 SERVINGS

- 2 tablespoons olive oil
- 1 beef brisket (3 to 4 pounds)

  Salt and black pepper
- 1 large onion, chopped
- 5 cloves garlic, minced
- 2 pounds Yukon Gold potatoes, cut into ¾-inch cubes
- 1 pound parsnips, cut into ¼-inch slices
- 1 pound carrots, cut into ¼-inch slices
- 1 cup dry red wine
- 1 cup beef broth
- ¼ cup tomato paste
- 1 teaspoon dried thyme
- 1 teaspoon dried rosemary
- 2 whole bay leaves

*Unless you have a 5-, 6- or 7-quart **CROCK-POT**® slow cooker, cut any roast larger than 2½ pounds in half so it cooks completely.*

1. Heat oil in large skillet over medium heat. Season brisket with salt and pepper. Brown brisket with onion and garlic about 2 to 3 minutes per side. Remove to **CROCK-POT**® slow cooker.

2. Add potatoes, parsnips, carrots, wine, broth, tomato paste, thyme, rosemary and bay leaves; stir to blend. Cover; cook on LOW 6 to 8 hours or on HIGH 4 to 6 hours.

3. Remove and discard bay leaves. Slice meat and serve with vegetables.

CHICKEN MEATBALLS IN SPICY TOMATO SAUCE

MAKES 4 SERVINGS

3 tablespoons olive oil, divided

1 medium onion, chopped

6 cloves garlic, minced

1½ teaspoons dried basil

¼ teaspoon red pepper flakes

2 cans (about 14 ounces *each*) diced tomatoes

3 tablespoons tomato paste

2 teaspoons salt, divided

1½ pounds ground chicken

2 egg yolks

1 teaspoon dried oregano

¼ teaspoon black pepper

1. Heat 2 tablespoons oil in large skillet over medium-high heat. Add onion, garlic, basil and red pepper flakes; cook and stir 5 minutes or until onion is softened. Remove half of mixture to **CROCK-POT**® slow cooker. Stir in diced tomatoes, tomato paste and 1 teaspoon salt.

2. Remove remaining onion mixture to large bowl. Add chicken, egg yolks, oregano, remaining 1 teaspoon salt and black pepper; mix well. Form mixture into 24 (1-inch) balls.

3. Heat remaining 1 tablespoon oil in large skillet. Add meatballs in batches; cook 7 minutes or until browned. Remove to **CROCK-POT**® slow cooker using slotted spoon. Cover; cook on LOW 4 to 5 hours.

BRAISED FRUITED LAMB

MAKES 6 TO 8 SERVINGS

6 tablespoons extra virgin olive oil

4 pounds lamb shanks

2 tablespoons salt

2 tablespoons black pepper

1 cup dried apricots

1 cup dried figs

1½ cups water

½ cup white vinegar or dry white wine

¼ cup raspberry jam

½ teaspoon ground allspice

½ teaspoon ground cinnamon

1. Preheat broiler. Brush oil on lamb shanks; season with salt and pepper. Place shanks on large baking sheet; broil 5 minutes per side. Remove to **CROCK-POT®** slow cooker. Add dried fruits.

2. Combine water, vinegar, jam, allspice and cinnamon in small bowl; stir to blend. Pour over lamb shanks. Cover; cook on LOW 8 to 9 hours or on HIGH 4 to 5 hours.

MIXED HERB AND BUTTER RUBBED CHICKEN

MAKES 4 TO 6 SERVINGS

3 tablespoons butter, softened

1 tablespoon grated lemon peel

2 teaspoons chopped fresh rosemary

1 teaspoon chopped fresh thyme

¾ teaspoon salt

¼ teaspoon black pepper

1 whole chicken (4½ to 5 pounds)

1. Coat inside of **CROCK-POT®** slow cooker with nonstick cooking spray. Combine butter, lemon peel, rosemary, thyme, salt and pepper in small bowl; stir to blend. Loosen skin over breast meat and drumsticks; pat chicken dry with paper towels. Rub butter mixture over and under chicken skin. Place chicken in **CROCK-POT®** slow cooker.

2. Cover; cook on LOW 5 to 6 hours, basting every 30 minutes with cooking liquid. Remove chicken to large cutting board. Let stand 15 minutes before cutting into pieces.

BEEF AND VEAL MEAT LOAF

MAKES 6 SERVINGS

- 1 tablespoon olive oil
- 1 small onion, chopped
- ½ red bell pepper, chopped
- 3 cloves garlic, minced
- 1 teaspoon dried oregano
- 1 pound ground beef
- 1 pound ground veal
- 1 egg
- 3 tablespoons tomato paste
- 1 teaspoon salt
- ½ teaspoon black pepper

1. Coat inside of **CROCK-POT**® slow cooker with nonstick cooking spray. Heat oil in large skillet over medium-high heat. Add onion, bell pepper, garlic and oregano; cook and stir 5 minutes or until vegetables are softened. Remove onion mixture to large bowl; cool 6 minutes.

2. Combine beef, veal, egg, tomato paste, salt and black pepper in large bowl with onion mixture; mix well. Form into 9×5-inch loaf; place in **CROCK-POT**® slow cooker.

3. Cover; cook on LOW 5 to 6 hours. Remove meat loaf to large cutting board; let stand 10 minutes before slicing.

PINEAPPLE AND BUTTERNUT SQUASH BRAISED CHICKEN

MAKES 4 SERVINGS

1 medium butternut squash, cut into 1-inch pieces (about 3 cups)

1 can (20 ounces) pineapple chunks, undrained

½ cup ketchup

8 chicken thighs (about 2 pounds)

½ teaspoon salt

¼ teaspoon black pepper

1. Coat inside of **CROCK-POT**® slow cooker with nonstick cooking spray. Combine squash, pineapple with juice and ketchup in **CROCK-POT**® slow cooker; stir to blend. Season chicken with salt and pepper. Place chicken on top of squash mixture.

2. Cover; cook on LOW 5 to 6 hours. Remove chicken to large platter; cover loosely with foil. Turn **CROCK-POT**® slow cooker to HIGH. Cook, uncovered, on HIGH 10 to 15 minutes or until sauce is thickened. Serve sauce over chicken.

# SIDES

BLUE CHEESE POTATOES

MAKES 5 SERVINGS

2 pounds red potatoes, peeled and cut into ½-inch pieces

1¼ cups chopped green onions, divided

2 tablespoons olive oil, divided

1 teaspoon dried basil

½ teaspoon salt

¼ teaspoon black pepper

½ cup crumbled blue cheese

1. Layer potatoes, 1 cup green onions, 1 tablespoon oil, basil, salt and pepper in **CROCK-POT**® slow cooker. Cover; cook on LOW 7 hours or on HIGH 4 hours.

2. Gently stir in cheese and remaining 1 tablespoon oil. Cover; cook on HIGH 5 minutes. Remove potatoes to large serving platter; top with remaining ¼ cup green onions.

SEASONED OKRA AND TOMATOES

MAKES 8 SERVINGS

1 tablespoon olive oil

1 medium onion, chopped

½ large green bell pepper, chopped

1 stalk celery, chopped

1 clove minced garlic

1 package (16 ounces) cut frozen okra, thawed

1 can (about 14 ounces) diced tomatoes, undrained

¾ teaspoon salt

½ teaspoon dried basil

½ teaspoon dried oregano

½ teaspoon black pepper

1. Heat oil in large skillet over medium-high heat. Add onion, bell pepper, celery and garlic; cook and stir 5 minutes or until onion is softened. Remove to **CROCK-POT** slow cooker using slotted spoon.

2. Stir in okra, tomatoes, salt, basil, oregano and black pepper. Cover; cook on LOW 2 hours.

ASIAN GOLDEN BARLEY WITH CASHEWS

MAKES 4 SERVINGS

2 tablespoons olive oil

1 cup hulled barley, sorted

3 cups vegetable broth

1 cup chopped celery

1 medium green bell pepper, chopped

1 medium yellow onion, chopped

1 clove garlic, minced

¼ teaspoon black pepper

Chopped cashew nuts

1. Heat large skillet over medium heat. Add oil and barley; cook and stir 10 minutes or until barley is slightly browned. Remove to **CROCK-POT**® slow cooker.

2. Add broth, celery, bell pepper, onion, garlic and black pepper; stir to blend. Cover; cook on LOW 4 to 5 hours or on HIGH 2 to 3 hours or until liquid is absorbed. Top with cashews.

MASHED RUTABAGAS AND POTATOES

MAKES 8 SERVINGS

2 pounds rutabagas, peeled and cut into ½-inch pieces

1 pound potatoes, peeled and cut into ½-inch pieces

½ cup milk

½ teaspoon ground nutmeg

2 tablespoons chopped fresh Italian parsley

Sprigs fresh Italian parsley (optional)

1. Place rutabagas and potatoes in **CROCK-POT®** slow cooker; add enough water to cover vegetables. Cover; cook on LOW 6 hours or on HIGH 3 hours. Remove vegetables to large bowl using slotted spoon. Discard cooking liquid.

2. Mash vegetables with potato masher. Add milk, nutmeg and chopped parsley; stir until smooth. Garnish with parsley sprigs.

SLOW-COOKED SUCCOTASH

MAKES 8 SERVINGS

2 teaspoons olive oil

1 cup diced onion

1 cup diced green bell pepper

1 cup diced celery

1 teaspoon paprika

1½ cups frozen corn

1½ cups frozen lima beans

1 cup canned diced tomatoes

1 tablespoon minced fresh Italian parsley

Salt and black pepper

1. Heat oil in large skillet over medium heat. Add onion, bell pepper and celery; cook and stir 5 minutes or until vegetables are crisp-tender. Stir in paprika.

2. Stir onion mixture, corn, beans, tomatoes, parsley, salt and black pepper into **CROCK-POT**® slow cooker. Cover; cook on LOW 6 to 8 hours or on HIGH 3 to 4 hours.

WHITE BEANS AND TOMATOES

MAKES 8 TO 10 SERVINGS

¼ cup olive oil

2 medium onions, chopped

1 tablespoon minced garlic

4 cups water

2 cans (about 14 ounces *each*) cannellini beans, rinsed and drained

1 can (about 28 ounces) crushed tomatoes

4 teaspoons dried oregano

2 teaspoons kosher salt

Black pepper (optional)

Sprigs fresh oregano (optional)

1. Heat oil in large skillet over medium heat. Add onions; cook 15 minutes or until tender and translucent, stirring occasionally. Add garlic; cook 1 minute.

2. Remove mixture to **CROCK-POT®** slow cooker. Add water, beans, tomatoes, dried oregano and salt. Cover; cook on LOW 8 hours or on HIGH 4 hours. Stir in pepper, if desired. Garnish with fresh oregano.

SLOW COOKER GREEN BEANS

MAKES 6 TO 8 SERVINGS

1 tablespoon olive oil

1 pound fresh green beans, trimmed and cut in half

1 teaspoon fresh garlic slivers

1½ cups beef broth

¾ cup water

¼ teaspoon black pepper

¼ cup (about 2 ounces) chopped pimientos

¼ cup sliced almonds*

To toast almonds, spread in single layer in heavy skillet. Cook and stir over medium heat 1 to 2 minutes or until nuts are lightly browned.

1. Heat oil in large skillet over high heat. Add beans; cook and stir 5 minutes or until beans begin to char and blister. Add garlic; cook 1 minute. Remove bean mixture to **CROCK-POT**® slow cooker.

2. Add broth, water, pepper and pimientos to **CROCK-POT**® slow cooker; stir to blend. Cover; cook on LOW 4 hours or on HIGH 2 hours. Sprinkle almonds over beans just before serving.

QUINOA PILAF WITH SHALLOT VINAIGRETTE

MAKES 6 SERVINGS

2 cups vegetable broth

1 cup uncooked quinoa, rinsed under cold running water

2 stalks celery, finely chopped

1 carrot, finely chopped

½ small red onion, finely chopped

¼ teaspoon dried thyme

1 medium shallot, chopped

1 tablespoon white wine vinegar

2 teaspoons honey

1 teaspoon Dijon mustard

⅛ teaspoon black pepper

¼ cup extra virgin olive oil

Chopped fresh Italian parsley (optional)

1. Combine broth, quinoa, celery, carrot, onion and thyme in **CROCK-POT**® slow cooker. Cover; cook on HIGH 2 to 3 hours or until liquid is absorbed.

2. Meanwhile, combine shallot, vinegar, honey, mustard and pepper in small bowl; whisk in oil. Fluff quinoa with fork; stir in shallot mixture. Garnish with parsley.

BALSAMIC-HONEY GLAZED ROOT VEGETABLES

MAKES 6 SERVINGS

4 medium carrots, cut into ½-inch pieces

2 medium parsnips, cut into ¾-inch pieces

1½ pounds sweet potatoes, peeled and cut into 1-inch pieces

2 medium red onions, each cut through root end into 6 wedges

¼ cup honey

3 tablespoons unsalted butter, melted

1 tablespoon balsamic vinegar

1 teaspoon salt

¼ teaspoon black pepper

1. Combine carrots, parsnips, sweet potatoes, onions, honey, butter, vinegar, salt and pepper in **CROCK-POT**® slow cooker; toss to coat vegetables. Cover; cook on LOW 4 to 5 hours or until vegetables are tender.

2. Remove vegetables to large bowl using slotted spoon. Turn **CROCK-POT**® slow cooker to HIGH. Cover; cook on HIGH 15 minutes or until sauce is thickened. Return vegetables to **CROCK-POT**® slow cooker; toss to coat.

BEETS IN SPICY MUSTARD SAUCE

MAKES 4 SERVINGS

3 pounds beets, peeled, halved and cut into ½-inch slices

¼ cup sour cream

2 tablespoons spicy brown mustard

2 teaspoons fresh lemon juice

2 cloves garlic, minced

¼ teaspoon black pepper

⅛ teaspoon dried thyme

1. Place beets in **CROCK-POT**® slow cooker. Add enough water to cover by 1 inch. Cover; cook on LOW 7 to 8 hours.

2. Combine sour cream, mustard, lemon juice, garlic, pepper and thyme in small bowl; stir to blend. Spoon over beets; toss to coat. Cover; cook on LOW 15 minutes.

OLIVE OIL MASHED RUTABAGAS

MAKES 8 SERVINGS

1 (2½- to 3-pound) rutabaga (waxed turnip), peeled and cut into 1-inch pieces

4 cloves garlic

Boiling water

2 tablespoons olive oil

1 teaspoon salt

1 teaspoon dried thyme

1. Combine rutabaga, garlic and enough boiling water to cover by 1 inch in **CROCK-POT®** slow cooker. Cover; cook on LOW 7 to 8 hours.

2. Place rutabaga in food processor or blender; purée, adding boiling water as necessary to reach desired consistency. Stir in oil, salt and thyme.

HARVARD BEETS ▶

MAKES 6 SERVINGS

2 pounds fresh beets, peeled and cut into 1-inch cubes

½ cup cider vinegar

⅓ cup honey

¼ cup water

1 teaspoon salt

1 tablespoon cornstarch

2 tablespoons butter

1. Place beets in **CROCK-POT®** slow cooker. Add vinegar, honey, water and salt; stir to blend. Cover; cook on HIGH 3 hours or until beets are just tender.

2. Remove 2 tablespoons juice from **CROCK-POT®** slow cooker to small bowl. Stir cornstarch into juice until smooth; whisk into **CROCK-POT®** slow cooker. Stir in butter. Cover; cook on HIGH 30 minutes.

BARLEY SALAD

MAKES 16 SERVINGS

2 onions, chopped

2 sweet potatoes, diced

1 cup pearl barley

1 teaspoon salt

½ teaspoon ground cinnamon

¼ teaspoon ground red pepper (optional)

1½ cups water

2 apples, peeled and chopped

1 cup dried cranberries

1 cup chopped pecans

1. Spread onions and potatoes on bottom of **CROCK-POT®** slow cooker. Add barley, salt, cinnamon and ground red pepper, if desired. Pour in water. Cook on LOW 4 hours or on HIGH 2 hours.

2. Stir in apples, cranberries and pecans. Serve warm or at room temperature.

HERBED FALL VEGETABLES

MAKES 6 SERVINGS

2 medium Yukon Gold potatoes, peeled and cut into ½-inch cubes

2 medium sweet potatoes, peeled and cut into ½-inch cubes

3 parsnips, cut into ½-inch cubes

1 fennel bulb, sliced and cut into ½-inch cubes

½ to ¾ cup chopped fresh herbs, such as tarragon, parsley, sage or thyme

¼ cup (½ stick) butter, cut into small pieces

1 cup chicken broth

1 tablespoon Dijon mustard

1 tablespoon salt

Black pepper

1. Combine potatoes, parsnips, fennel, herbs and butter in **CROCK-POT**® slow cooker.

2. Whisk broth, mustard, salt and pepper in small bowl. Pour mixture over vegetables. Cover; cook on LOW 4½ hours or on HIGH 3 hours or until vegetables are tender, stirring occasionally.

HOT THREE-BEAN CASSEROLE

MAKES 12 SERVINGS

2 tablespoons olive oil

1 cup coarsely chopped onion

1 cup chopped celery

2 cloves garlic, minced

1 can (about 15 ounces) chickpeas, rinsed and drained

1 can (about 15 ounces) kidney beans, rinsed and drained

1 package (10 ounces) frozen cut green beans

1 cup water

1 cup coarsely chopped tomato

1 can (8 ounces) tomato sauce

1 to 2 jalapeño peppers, seeded and minced*

1 tablespoon chili powder

1½ teaspoons ground cumin

1 teaspoon salt

1 teaspoon dried oregano

¼ teaspoon black pepper

Sprigs fresh oregano (optional)

*Jalapeño peppers can sting and irritate the skin, so wear rubber gloves when handling peppers and do not touch your eyes.

1. Heat oil in large skillet over medium heat. Add onion, celery and garlic; cook and stir 5 minutes or until tender. Remove to **CROCK-POT®** slow cooker.

2. Add chickpeas, beans, water, tomato, tomato sauce, jalapeño pepper, chili powder, cumin, salt, dried oregano and black pepper to **CROCK-POT®** slow cooker; stir to blend. Cover; cook on LOW 6 to 8 hours. Garnish with fresh oregano.

COLLARD GREENS

MAKES 6 SERVINGS

- 1 tablespoon olive oil
- 3 turkey necks
- 5 bunches collard greens, stemmed and chopped
- 5 cups chicken broth
- 1 small onion, chopped
- 2 cloves garlic, minced
- 1 tablespoon cider vinegar
- Salt and black pepper
- Red pepper flakes

1. Heat oil in large skillet over medium-high heat. Add turkey necks; cook and stir 3 to 5 minutes or until brown.

2. Combine turkey necks, collard greens, broth, onion and garlic in **CROCK-POT®** slow cooker. Cover; cook on LOW 5 to 6 hours. Remove and discard turkey necks. Stir in vinegar, salt, black pepper and red pepper flakes.

CONFETTI BLACK BEANS

MAKES 6 SERVINGS

1 cup dried black beans, rinsed and sorted

1½ teaspoons olive oil

1 medium onion, chopped

¼ cup chopped red bell pepper

¼ cup chopped yellow bell pepper

1 jalapeño pepper, finely chopped*

1 large tomato, chopped

½ teaspoon salt

⅛ teaspoon black pepper

2 cloves garlic, minced

1 can (about 14 ounces) chicken broth

1 whole bay leaf

Hot pepper sauce (optional)

Jalapeño peppers can sting and irritate the skin, so wear rubber gloves when handling peppers and do not touch your eyes.

1. Place beans in large bowl and add enough cold water to cover by at least 2 inches. Soak 6 to 8 hours or overnight.** Drain beans; discard water.

2. Heat oil in large skillet over medium heat. Add onion, bell peppers and jalapeño pepper; cook and stir 5 minutes or until onion is tender. Add tomato, salt and black pepper; cook 5 minutes. Stir in garlic.

3. Place beans, broth and bay leaf in **CROCK-POT**® slow cooker. Add onion mixture. Cover; cook on LOW 7 to 8 hours or on HIGH 4½ to 5 hours. Remove and discard bay leaf. Serve with hot pepper sauce, if desired.

**To quick soak beans, place beans in large saucepan; cover with water. Bring to a boil over high heat. Boil 2 minutes. Remove from heat; let soak, covered, 1 hour.

INDEX

A

Almonds

Caribbean Sweet Potato and Bean Stew, 88

Jamaican Quinoa and Sweet Potato Stew, 106

Overnight Breakfast Porridge, 16

Slow Cooker Green Beans, 168

Whoa Breakfast, 11

Apple

Barley Salad, 178

Mulled Cran-Apple Juice, 18

Oatmeal with Maple-Glazed Apples and Cranberries, 20

Spiced Apple Tea, 22

Spiced Vanilla Applesauce, 36

Whoa Breakfast, 11

Artichokes

Spinach Artichoke Gratin, 104

Steamed Artichokes with Three Sauces, 116

Asian Golden Barley with Cashews, 160

Asian Kale and Chickpeas, 98

Asian Pork Tenderloin, 140

B

Balsamic-Honey Glazed Root Vegetables, 172

Bananas: Hawaiian Fruit Compote, 40

Barley

Asian Golden Barley with Cashews, 160

Barley and Vegetable Risotto, 90

Barley Salad, 178

Barley with Currants and Pine Nuts, 86

Mushroom Barley Stew, 112

Turkey Breast with Barley-Cranberry Stuffing, 126

Barley and Vegetable Risotto, 90

Barley Salad, 178

Barley with Currants and Pine Nuts, 86

Basque Chicken with Peppers, 134

Beans, Black

Beef Fajita Soup, 78

Black Bean Mushroom Chili, 56

Black Bean Stuffed Peppers, 102

Caribbean Sweet Potato and Bean Stew, 88

Confetti Black Beans, 186

Fresh Lime and Black Bean Soup, 70

Pork Tenderloin Chili, 46

Southwestern Stuffed Peppers, 82

Three-Bean Turkey Chili, 64

Beans, Cannellini

Curried Lamb and Swiss Chard Soup, 58

Italian Escarole and White Bean Stew, 96

Italian-Style Pot Roast, 120

Northwest Beef and Vegetable Soup, 66

Savory Chicken and Oregano Chili, 68

White Bean Chili, 74

White Beans and Tomatoes, 166

Beans, Green

Caribbean Sweet Potato and Bean Stew, 88

Hearty Lentil Stew, 84

Hot Three-Bean Casserole, 182

Slow Cooker Green Beans, 168

Thai Red Curry with Tofu, 114

Beans, Kidney

Hot Three-Bean Casserole, 182

Simple Beef Chili, 43

Three-Bean Turkey Chili, 64

Beans, Lima: Slow-Cooked Succotash, 164

Beans, Navy

Chunky Italian Stew with White Beans, 92

White Chicken Chili, 52

Beans, Pinto

Beef Fajita Soup, 78

Pork Tenderloin Chili, 46

Beef

Beef and Beet Borscht, 48

Beef Fajita Soup, 78

Braised Beef Brisket, 144

Braised Chipotle Beef, 138

Brisket with Sweet Onions, 130

Italian-Style Pot Roast, 120

Northwest Beef and Vegetable Soup, 66

Thai Steak Salad, 128

Beef and Beet Borscht, 48

Beef and Veal Meat Loaf, 152

Beef Fajita Soup, 78

Beef, Ground

Beef and Veal Meat Loaf, 152

Simple Beef Chili, 43

Beets

Beef and Beet Borscht, 48

Beets in Spicy Mustard Sauce, 174

Harvard Beets, 178

Beets in Spicy Mustard Sauce, 174

Berry

Barley Salad, 178

Four Fruit Oatmeal, 24

Mulled Cran-Apple Juice, 18

Oatmeal with Maple-Glazed Apples and Cranberries, 20

Overnight Breakfast Porridge, 16

Turkey Breast with Barley-Cranberry Stuffing, 126

Beverages

Ginger Pear Cider, 12

Mulled Cran-Apple Juice, 18

Spiced Apple Tea, 22

Spiced Citrus Tea, 32

Black Bean Mushroom Chili, 56

Black Bean Stuffed Peppers, 102

Blue Cheese Potatoes, 157

Boneless Pork Roast with Garlic, 122

Braised Beef Brisket, 144

Braised Chipotle Beef, 138

Braised Fruited Lamb, 148

Braised Sea Bass with Aromatic Vegetables, 132

Bran Muffin Bread, 26

Breakfast Quinoa, 34

Brisket with Sweet Onions, 130

Butternut Squash, Chickpea and Lentil Stew, 100

C

Cabbage

Beef and Beet Borscht, 48

Curried Lamb and Swiss Chard Soup, 58

Thai Steak Salad, 128

Caribbean Sweet Potato and Bean Stew, 88

Carrots

Balsamic-Honey Glazed Root Vegetables, 172

Beef and Beet Borscht, 48

Braised Beef Brisket, 144

Braised Sea Bass with Aromatic Vegetables, 132

Chicken and Vegetable Soup, 50

Hearty Lentil Stew, 84

Italian Escarole and White Bean Stew, 96

Lentil and Portobello Soup, 54

Mushroom Barley Stew, 112

Quinoa Pilaf with Shallot Vinaigrette, 170

Cauliflower

Cauliflower Soup, 62

Hearty Lentil Stew, 84

Cauliflower Soup, 62

Cherries

Four Fruit Oatmeal, 24

Hawaiian Fruit Compote, 40

Chicken

Basque Chicken with Peppers, 134

Chicken and Butternut Squash, 119

Chicken and Vegetable Soup, 50

Chicken Meatballs in Spicy Tomato Sauce, 146

Jamaica-Me-Crazy Chicken Tropicale, 124

Mixed Herb and Butter Rubbed Chicken, 150

Pineapple and Butternut Squash Braised Chicken, 154

Savory Chicken and Oregano Chili, 68

White Bean Chili, 74

White Chicken Chili, 52

Chicken and Butternut Squash, 119

Chicken and Vegetable Soup, 50

Chicken Meatballs in Spicy Tomato Sauce, 146

Chickpeas

Asian Kale and Chickpeas, 98

Butternut Squash, Chickpea and Lentil Stew, 100

Hot Three-Bean Casserole, 182

Summer Vegetable Stew, 108

Three-Bean Turkey Chili, 64

Chunky Italian Stew with White Beans, 92

Collard Greens, 184

Confetti Black Beans, 186

Corn

Simple Beef Chili, 43

Slow-Cooked Succotash, 164

Southwestern Stuffed Peppers, 82

Summer Vegetable Stew, 108

Cream Cheese Dipping Sauce, 116

Creamy Sweet Potato and Butternut Squash Soup, 72

Cucumber: Simple Salmon with Fresh Salsa, 142

Curried Lamb and Swiss Chard Soup, 58

E

Egg Dishes

Hash Brown and Spinach Breakfast Casserole, 38

Mediterranean Frittata, 14

Wake-Up Potato and Sausage Breakfast Casserole, 30

Eggplant

Quinoa and Vegetable Medley, 110

Ratatouille with Parmesan Cheese, 94

Thai Red Curry with Tofu, 114

Escarole: Italian Escarole and White Bean Stew, 96

F

Four Fruit Oatmeal, 24

Fresh Lime and Black Bean Soup, 70

G

Garlic-Herb Butter Dipping Sauce, 117

Garlic Lentil Soup with Mushrooms and Greens, 44

Ginger Pear Cider, 12

H

Harvard Beets, 178

Hash Brown and Spinach Breakfast Casserole, 38

Hawaiian Fruit Compote, 40

Hearty Lentil Stew, 84

Hearty Vegetarian Mac and Cheese, 81

Herbed Fall Vegetables, 180

Honey

Balsamic-Honey Glazed Root Vegetables, 172

Ginger Pear Cider, 12

Harvard Beets, 178

Hot Three-Bean Casserole, 182

I

Italian Escarole and White Bean Stew, 96

Italian-Style Pot Roast, 120

J

Jamaica-Me-Crazy Chicken Tropicale, 124

Jamaican Quinoa and Sweet Potato Stew, 106

K

Kale

Asian Kale and Chickpeas, 98

Garlic Lentil Soup with Mushrooms and Greens, 44

L

Lamb

Braised Fruited Lamb, 148

Curried Lamb and Swiss Chard Soup, 58

Leeks: Braised Sea Bass with Aromatic Vegetables, 132

Lentil and Portobello Soup, 54

INDEX

Lentils
Butternut Squash, Chickpea and Lentil Stew, 100
Garlic Lentil Soup with Mushrooms and Greens, 44
Hearty Lentil Stew, 84
Lentil and Portobello Soup, 54

M
Mango
Hawaiian Fruit Compote, 40
Thai Steak Salad, 128

Maple
Breakfast Quinoa, 34
Mulled Cran-Apple Juice, 18
Oatmeal with Maple-Glazed Apples and Cranberries, 20
Mashed Rutabagas and Potatoes, 162
Mediterranean Frittata, 14
Mixed Herb and Butter Rubbed Chicken, 150
Mulled Cran-Apple Juice, 18
Mushroom Barley Stew, 112

Mushrooms
Barley and Vegetable Risotto, 90
Basque Chicken with Peppers, 134
Black Bean Mushroom Chili, 56
Chunky Italian Stew with White Beans, 92
Garlic Lentil Soup with Mushrooms and Greens, 44
Hash Brown and Spinach Breakfast Casserole, 38
Lentil and Portobello Soup, 54
Mediterranean Frittata, 14
Mushroom Barley Stew, 112
Mushroom Soup, 76
Ratatouille with Parmesan Cheese, 94
Mushroom Soup, 76

N
Northwest Beef and Vegetable Soup, 66

O
Oatmeal with Maple-Glazed Apples and Cranberries, 20

Oats
Four Fruit Oatmeal, 24
Oatmeal with Maple-Glazed Apples and Cranberries, 20
Overnight Breakfast Porridge, 16
Whoa Breakfast, 11
Old-Fashioned Split Pea Soup, 60
Olive Oil Mashed Rutabagas, 176
Olives: Mediterranean Frittata, 14

Orange
Mulled Cran-Apple Juice, 18
Spiced Citrus Tea, 32
Overnight Breakfast Porridge, 16

P
Parsnips
Balsamic-Honey Glazed Root Vegetables, 172
Braised Beef Brisket, 144
Chicken and Vegetable Soup, 50
Herbed Fall Vegetables, 180
Peaches: Hawaiian Fruit Compote, 40

Peanuts
Hearty Lentil Stew, 84
Thai Steak Salad, 128

Pear
Ginger Pear Cider, 12
Pear Crunch, 28
Pear Crunch, 28
Pecans: Barley Salad, 178
Peppers, Bell
Asian Golden Barley with Cashews, 160
Asian Pork Tenderloin, 140
Barley and Vegetable Risotto, 90
Basque Chicken with Peppers, 134
Beef and Veal Meat Loaf, 152
Beef Fajita Soup, 78
Black Bean Mushroom Chili, 56
Black Bean Stuffed Peppers, 102
Braised Chipotle Beef, 138

Chunky Italian Stew with White Beans, 92
Confetti Black Beans, 186
Jamaican Quinoa and Sweet Potato Stew, 106
Mediterranean Frittata, 14
Quinoa and Vegetable Medley, 110
Savory Chicken and Oregano Chili, 68
Seasoned Okra and Tomatoes, 158
Simple Beef Chili, 43
Simple Salmon with Fresh Salsa, 142
Slow-Cooked Succotash, 164
Southwestern Stuffed Peppers, 82
Thai Red Curry with Tofu, 114
Wake-Up Potato and Sausage Breakfast Casserole, 30

Pineapple
Hawaiian Fruit Compote, 40
Jamaica-Me-Crazy Chicken Tropicale, 124
Pear Crunch, 28
Pineapple and Butternut Squash Braised Chicken, 154
Pineapple and Butternut Squash Braised Chicken, 154
Pine Nuts: Barley with Currants and Pine Nuts, 86
Pork
Asian Pork Tenderloin, 140
Boneless Pork Roast with Garlic, 122
Pork Tenderloin Chili, 46
Pork Tenderloin Chili, 46
Potatoes
Blue Cheese Potatoes, 157
Braised Beef Brisket, 144
Hash Brown and Spinach Breakfast Casserole, 38
Herbed Fall Vegetables, 180
Mashed Rutabagas and Potatoes, 162
Northwest Beef and Vegetable Soup, 66
Wake-Up Potato and Sausage Breakfast Casserole, 30

Potatoes, Sweet
Balsamic-Honey Glazed Root Vegetables, 172
Barley Salad, 178
Caribbean Sweet Potato and Bean Stew, 88
Creamy Sweet Potato and Butternut Squash Soup, 72
Herbed Fall Vegetables, 180
Jamaica-Me-Crazy Chicken Tropicale, 124
Jamaican Quinoa and Sweet Potato Stew, 106
Quinoa and Vegetable Medley, 110
Thai Red Curry with Tofu, 114

Q
Quinoa
Breakfast Quinoa, 34
Jamaican Quinoa and Sweet Potato Stew, 106
Overnight Breakfast Porridge, 16
Quinoa and Vegetable Medley, 110
Quinoa Pilaf with Shallot Vinaigrette, 170
Quinoa and Vegetable Medley, 110
Quinoa Pilaf with Shallot Vinaigrette, 170

R
Raisins
Bran Muffin Bread, 26
Breakfast Quinoa, 34
Four Fruit Oatmeal, 24
Jamaica-Me-Crazy Chicken Tropicale, 124
Overnight Breakfast Porridge, 16
Ratatouille with Parmesan Cheese, 94
Rice, Brown: Southwestern Stuffed Peppers, 82
Rutabagas
Mashed Rutabagas and Potatoes, 162
Olive Oil Mashed Rutabagas, 176

S
Salsa
Black Bean Mushroom Chili, 56
Black Bean Stuffed Peppers, 102
Southwestern Stuffed Peppers, 82
Savory Chicken and Oregano Chili, 68
Seafood
Braised Sea Bass with Aromatic Vegetables, 132
Simple Salmon with Fresh Salsa, 142
Seasoned Okra and Tomatoes, 158
Simple Beef Chili, 43
Simple Salmon with Fresh Salsa, 142
Slow-Cooked Succotash, 164
Slow Cooker Green Beans, 168
Southwestern Stuffed Peppers, 82
Spiced Apple Tea, 22
Spiced Citrus Tea, 32
Spiced Vanilla Applesauce, 36
Spicy Turkey with Citrus au Jus, 136
Spinach
Barley and Vegetable Risotto, 90
Hash Brown and Spinach Breakfast Casserole, 38
Mediterranean Frittata, 14
Spinach Artichoke Gratin, 104
Spinach Artichoke Gratin, 104
Squash
Asian Pork Tenderloin, 140
Butternut Squash, Chickpea and Lentil Stew, 100
Chicken and Butternut Squash, 119
Chunky Italian Stew with White Beans, 92
Creamy Sweet Potato and Butternut Squash Soup, 72
Northwest Beef and Vegetable Soup, 66
Pineapple and Butternut Squash Braised Chicken, 154

Ratatouille with Parmesan Cheese, 94
Summer Vegetable Stew, 108
Steamed Artichokes with Three Sauces, 116
Summer Vegetable Stew, 108
Swiss Chard: Curried Lamb and Swiss Chard Soup, 58
T
Tarragon Browned Butter Dipping Sauce, 116
Thai Red Curry with Tofu, 114
Thai Steak Salad, 128
Three-Bean Turkey Chili, 64
Tofu: Thai Red Curry with Tofu, 114
Tomatoes, Fresh
Confetti Black Beans, 186
Hot Three-Bean Casserole, 182
Quinoa and Vegetable Medley, 110
Ratatouille with Parmesan Cheese, 94
Simple Salmon with Fresh Salsa, 142
Summer Vegetable Stew, 108
Turkey
Collard Greens, 184
Spicy Turkey with Citrus au Jus, 136
Three-Bean Turkey Chili, 64
Turkey Breast with Barley-Cranberry Stuffing, 126
Turkey Breast with Barley-Cranberry Stuffing, 126
Turnips: Northwest Beef and Vegetable Soup, 66
V
Veal: Beef and Veal Meat Loaf, 152
W
Wake-Up Potato and Sausage Breakfast Casserole, 30
Walnuts: Bran Muffin Bread, 26
White Bean Chili, 74
White Beans and Tomatoes, 166
White Chicken Chili, 52
Whoa Breakfast, 11

METRIC CONVERSION CHART

VOLUME MEASUREMENTS (dry)

1/8 teaspoon = 0.5 mL
1/4 teaspoon = 1 mL
1/2 teaspoon = 2 mL
3/4 teaspoon = 4 mL
1 teaspoon = 5 mL
1 tablespoon = 15 mL
2 tablespoons = 30 mL
1/4 cup = 60 mL
1/3 cup = 75 mL
1/2 cup = 125 mL
2/3 cup = 150 mL
3/4 cup = 175 mL
1 cup = 250 mL
2 cups = 1 pint = 500 mL
3 cups = 750 mL
4 cups = 1 quart = 1 L

VOLUME MEASUREMENTS (fluid)

1 fluid ounce (2 tablespoons) = 30 mL
4 fluid ounces (1/2 cup) = 125 mL
8 fluid ounces (1 cup) = 250 mL
12 fluid ounces (1 1/2 cups) = 375 mL
16 fluid ounces (2 cups) = 500 mL

WEIGHTS (mass)

1/2 ounce = 15 g
1 ounce = 30 g
3 ounces = 90 g
4 ounces = 120 g
8 ounces = 225 g
10 ounces = 285 g
12 ounces = 360 g
16 ounces = 1 pound = 450 g

DIMENSIONS

1/16 inch = 2 mm
1/8 inch = 3 mm
1/4 inch = 6 mm
1/2 inch = 1.5 cm
3/4 inch = 2 cm
1 inch = 2.5 cm

OVEN TEMPERATURES

250°F = 120°C
275°F = 140°C
300°F = 150°C
325°F = 160°C
350°F = 180°C
375°F = 190°C
400°F = 200°C
425°F = 220°C
450°F = 230°C

BAKING PAN SIZES

Utensil	Size in Inches/Quarts	Metric Volume	Size in Centimeters
Baking or Cake Pan (square or rectangular)	8×8×2	2 L	20×20×5
	9×9×2	2.5 L	23×23×5
	12×8×2	3 L	30×20×5
	13×9×2	3.5 L	33×23×5
Loaf Pan	8×4×3	1.5 L	20×10×7
	9×5×3	2 L	23×13×7
Round Layer Cake Pan	8×1½	1.2 L	20×4
	9×1½	1.5 L	23×4
Pie Plate	8×1¼	750 mL	20×3
	9×1¼	1 L	23×3
Baking Dish or Casserole	1 quart	1 L	—
	1½ quart	1.5 L	—
	2 quart	2 L	—